Excel

Get the Results You Want!

Year 2 NAPLAN*-style Literacy Tests

Tanya Dalgleish

PASCAL PRESS

* This is not an officially endorsed publication of the NAPLAN program and is produced by Pascal Press independently of Australian governments.

Conventions of Language questions updated 2017

Revised in 2020 for the NAPLAN Online tests

Reprinted 2020, 2022, 2023, 2024, 2025

ISBN 978 1 74125 451 8

Pascal Press Pty Ltd
PO Box 250
Glebe NSW 2037
www.pascalpress.com.au

Publisher: Vivienne Joannou
Project editor: Rosemary Peers
Edited by Rosemary Peers
Answers checked by Valerie McCool and Dale Little
Cover and page design by DiZign Pty Ltd
Typesetting by DiZign Pty Ltd and lj Design (Julianne Billington)
Printed by Vivar Printing/Green Giant Press

Contents

NAPLAN AND NAPLAN ONLINE

WHAT IS NAPLAN?

- NAPLAN stands for National Assessment Program—Literacy and Numeracy.
- It is conducted every year in March and the tests are taken by students in Years 3, 5, 7 and 9.
- The tests cover Literacy—Reading, Writing, Conventions of Language (spelling, grammar and punctuation)—and Numeracy.

WHAT IS NAPLAN ONLINE?

Introduction

- In the past all NAPLAN tests were paper tests.
- From 2022 all students have taken the NAPLAN tests online.
- This means students complete the NAPLAN tests on a computer or tablet.

Tailored test design

- With NAPLAN paper tests, all students in each year level took exactly the same tests.
- In the NAPLAN Online tests this isn't the case; instead, every student takes a tailor-made test based on their ability.
- Please visit the official ACARA site for a detailed explanation of the tailored test process used in NAPLAN Online and also for general information about the tests: https://nap.edu.au/online-assessment.
- These tailor-made tests mean broadly, therefore, that a student who is at a standard level of achievement takes a test mostly comprised of questions of a standard level; a student who is at an intermediate level of achievement takes a test mostly comprised of questions of an intermediate level; and a student who is at an advanced level of achievement takes a test mostly comprised of questions of an advanced level.

Different question types

- Because of the digital format, NAPLAN Online contains more question types than in the paper tests. In the paper tests there are only multiple-choice and short-answer question types. In NAPLAN Online, however, there are also other question types. For example, students might be asked to drag text across a screen or listen to an audio recording of a sentence and then spell a word they hear.
- Please refer to the next page to see some examples of these additional question types that are found in NAPLAN Online and how they compare to questions in this book. As you will see, the content tested is exactly the same but the questions are presented differently.

NAPLAN ONLINE QUESTION TYPES

Additional NAPLAN Online question types	Equivalent questions in this book
Drag and drop Drag the correct word to fill the space. were was has is The children ______ quiet.	Which word correctly completes this sentence? The children ______ quiet. **A** were **B** was **C** has **D** is
Draw lines Match the adjectives to the nouns. Click then drag to draw lines between them. dry — skin noisy — clothes soft — tree tall — magpies	Draw lines to connect the adjectives to the correct nouns. dry — skin noisy — clothes soft — tree tall — magpies
Text entry Worms are good for the ______. Click on the play button to listen to the missing word. 0.08 / 0.09 Type the correct spelling of the word in the box.	Ask your teacher or parent to read the spelling words for you. The words are listed on page 129. Write the spelling word on the line below. Word: garden — Example: Worms are good for the garden. ______
Click A full stop (.) is missing from this sentence. Click to mark where the full stop should go. We had pasta with prawns for dinner	A full stop (.) is missing from this sentence. Where does the missing full stop go? We had (A) pasta (B) with prawns (C) for dinner (D)
Order Drag the sentences to put them in the correct order for events in the text. The queen lays eggs. Adult wasps emerge from cells. Larvae grow into pupae stage. Larvae hatch from the eggs.	Write the numbers 1 to 4 in the boxes to show the order of events in the text. The first one [1] has been done for you. [1] The queen lays eggs. [ ] Adult wasps emerge from cells. [ ] Larvae grow into pupae stage. [ ] Larvae hatch from the eggs.

MAXIMISE YOUR RESULTS IN NAPLAN ONLINE

STEP 1: USE THIS BOOK

How *Excel* can help you prepare for NAPLAN Online

Tailored test design

- We can't replicate the digital experience in book form and offer you tailored tests, but with this series we do provide Standard, Intermediate and Advanced NAPLAN Online–style Literacy tests—both mini tests and the longer sample tests.
- This means that a student using these tests will be able to prepare with confidence for tests at different ability levels.
- This makes it excellent preparation for the tailored NAPLAN Online Literacy tests.

Remember the advantages of revising in book form

There are many benefits to a child using books to prepare for the online test:

- One of the most important benefits is that writing on paper will help your child retain information. It can be a very effective way to memorise. High-quality educational research has shown that writing by hand is more effective than using a keyboard for remembering what you write and assisting in learning.
- Students will be able to prepare thoroughly for topic revision using books and then practise computer skills easily. They will only succeed with sound knowledge of topics; this requires study and focus. Students will not succeed in tests simply because they know how to answer questions digitally.
- Some students find it easier to concentrate when reading a page in a book than when reading on a screen.
- It can be more convenient to use a book, especially when a child doesn't have ready access to a digital device.
- You can be confident that ***Excel*** books will help students acquire the topic knowledge they need, as we have over 30 years experience in helping students prepare for tests. All our writers are experienced educators.

STEP 2: PRACTISE ON *Excel Test Zone*

How *Excel Test Zone* can help you practise online

We recommend you go to www.exceltestzone.com.au and register for practice in NAPLAN Online–style tests once you have completed this book. The reasons include:

- for optimal performance in the NAPLAN Online tests we recommend students gain practice at completing online tests as well as completing revision in book form
- students should practise answering questions on a digital device to become confident with this process
- students will be able to practise tailored tests like those in NAPLAN Online, as well as other types of tests
- students will also be able to gain valuable practice in onscreen skills such as dragging and dropping answers, using an online ruler to measure figures and using an online protractor to measure angles.

Remember that ***Excel Test Zone*** has been helping students prepare for NAPLAN since 2009; in fact we had NAPLAN online questions even before NAPLAN tests went online!

We also have updated our website along with our book range to ensure your preparation for NAPLAN Online is 100% up to date.

ABOUT THE LITERACY TESTS AND THIS BOOK

THE YEAR 3 NAPLAN LITERACY TESTS

Please note there are no Year 2 NAPLAN tests. This book will help you prepare for the Year 3 NAPLAN Literacy tests a year early, so you can get a head start!

About the tests

In Literacy there are three NAPLAN tests:

- **Reading** (comprehension)—there are 39 questions in this test
- **Conventions of Language** (spelling, grammar and punctuation)—there are 50 questions in this test
- **Writing** (written expression)—there is one piece of writing in this test.

About the report

- When your child completes the NAPLAN tests, you and your child's school will receive a report indicating their standard of proficiency in literacy and numeracy. There are four levels of achievement:
  - **Exceeding** (advanced proficiency)
  - **Strong** (average to high-average proficiency)
  - **Developing** (not yet proficient)
  - **Needs additional support** (help is needed).

The report will also show the national average.

ABOUT THIS BOOK

The Mini Reading and Conventions of Language Tests

In the first part of the book you will find ten tests for each subject. These tests are divided into three levels of difficulty:

- Standard level
- Intermediate level
- Advanced level.

- You will be able to see what level your child is at by finding the point where he or she starts having consistent difficulty with questions. For example, if your child answers most questions correctly up to the intermediate level and then gets most questions wrong from then onwards, it is likely your child's ability is at an intermediate level.
- You will be able to see your child's strengths and weaknesses in different topics by completing the **Strengths and weaknesses chart** (see page viii).
- You will also be able to give your child intensive practice in short tests which have time limits based on the actual Reading and Conventions of Language test times.
- There are quick answers for every question so you can easily mark your child's work.
- For the **Reading tests**, line references and explanations are provided. The line references will help you find exactly where the answer to the question is found in the text. Questions in the reading answer section have been divided into five types: fact-finding, inferring, judgement, language and synthesis. Explanations are provided within these answer scaffolds to help you teach your child how to answer the different types of reading questions. If you turn to the inside back cover you will see all these types of explanations explained fully.
- For the **Conventions of Language tests**, tips and explanations are provided. Your child can then learn to apply these general tips to similar questions and the explanations will help you to explain the answers to your child.

The Mini Writing Tests

- There are three Writing tests.
- There are tips specific to the type of text of the questions. These tips will provide guidelines for your child's writing.
- Each Writing test has writing samples at an intermediate and advanced level. From these you will be able to see the level at which your child is writing. For example, if your child's writing closely resembles the intermediate writing sample then their writing is at the intermediate level.
- Marking checklists are also provided so you can go through your child's writing and check that they have covered all the points.

The Sample Literacy Tests

- In the second part of the book we provide you with three sample tests.
- Your child will be able to practise the longer sample tests.
- For the Conventions of Language and Reading tests there are answers, tips and explanations, and also a list of each question's level of difficulty to help you identify which are the easier and harder questions in the tests.
- For the Writing tests there are marking checklists and writing samples, one each of an intermediate and advanced level. From these you will be able to see which level your child is writing at by comparing their writing to the writing samples.

STRENGTHS AND WEAKNESSES CHART

- As your child completes each test, mark it using the answer section at the back and then fill in this chart to record their progress.
- You will be able to see at a glance your child's strengths and weaknesses in different topics and different strands of Literacy.
- If you find your child needs more practice on specific topics, use the checklist of ***Excel*** books on the back cover to find the book to help them.

Area of Learning	Level	Mini Test	Mark
Spelling	Standard	1	/18
Spelling	Standard	2	/18
Spelling	Intermediate	3	/18
Spelling	Intermediate	4	/18
Spelling	Intermediate	5	/18
Spelling	Intermediate	6	/18
Spelling	Advanced	7	/18
Spelling	Advanced	8	/18
Spelling	Advanced	9	/18
Spelling	Advanced	10	/18
Grammar	Standard	1	/18
Grammar	Intermediate	2	/18
Grammar	Intermediate	3	/18
Grammar	Advanced	4	/18
Grammar	Advanced	5	/18
Punctuation	Standard	1	/18
Punctuation	Intermediate	2	/18
Punctuation	Intermediate	3	/18
Punctuation	Advanced	4	/18
Punctuation	Advanced	5	/18
Reading	Standard	1	/6
Reading	Standard	2	/6
Reading	Intermediate	3	/6
Reading	Intermediate	4	/6
Reading	Intermediate	5	/6
Reading	Intermediate	6	/6
Reading	Advanced	7	/6
Reading	Advanced	8	/6
Reading	Advanced	9	/6
Reading	Advanced	10	/6

SPELLING

Standard level questions

Mini Test 1

The spelling mistakes in these sentences have been highlighted. Write the correct spelling for each highlighted word in the box.

1 The children had to stand in to lines.

2 We stood outside the clarsroom.

3 Yoo can have the next turn.

4 The teacher told us to poot down our pencils.

5 The teacher said to rite a story.

6 Our ball whent under the house.

7 I liek Ben's kitten.

8 Mum sed I can have a goldfish.

9 My dog's naym is Scruff.

10 We rode our bikes to the parck.

The spelling mistakes in these labels have been highlighted. Write the correct spelling for each highlighted word in the box.

11 egz

12 nesst

13 berd

Read the text *Bees*. The spelling mistake in each line has been highlighted. Write the correct spelling for each highlighted word in the box.

Bees

14 A bee is an inseckt.

15 Bees live in a hiv .

16 Bees gatha pollen and nectar from flowers.

17 Thay take the nectar to their hive.

18 Bees use the nectar to mak honey.

Answers and explanations on page 84

SPELLING

Standard level questions

Mini Test 2

Each line has a word that is incorrect. Write the correct spelling of the word in the box.

1 My aunt just had a baby and it's a gerl.

2 There are ten boiz in the class.

3 The kitten was aslepe.

4 Thiss apple is really sweet.

5 Tooday is Monday.

6 The teacher said to run around the oval agen.

7 The tiny littel puppy was crying.

8 Stop, luk and listen before you cross the road.

9 John showed Jason howe to play the game.

10 We can eat the cake wen it cools.

The words below are in pairs where the words go together. In each pair one word is spelt incorrectly. Write the correct spelling of the word in the box.

11 for flies three flies

12 one foot two foots

13 one finga one hand

Read the text *At the beach*. Each line has a word that is incorrect. Write the correct spelling of the word in the box.

At the beach

14 It was a lovely suny day.

15 We caught the buss to school.

16 The warter was too cold for swimming.

17 My sister and I climbed ova the rocks.

18 We saw krabs in a rock pool.

Answers and explanations on pages 84–85

SPELLING

Intermediate level questions

Mini Test 3

The spelling mistakes in these sentences have been highlighted. Write the correct spelling for each highlighted word in the box.

1 Tim loves going to the **beech**.

2 Sara's dad is a **plice** officer.

3 Henry **puled** the weeds from Grandma's garden.

4 **Owr** computer broke down.

5 Mum said to take the muddy dog **owtside**.

6 Milly was **sloh** to eat her lunch.

7 Mindy came first in the **runing** race.

8 I brushed my **teef** before bed.

9 Dad said to make a **whish** when you see a shooting star.

10 Tomorrow is a **skool** day.

The spelling mistakes in these labels have been highlighted. Write the correct spelling for each highlighted word in the box.

11 **dor**

12 **chere**

13 **tabel**

Read the text *Menu*. The spelling mistake in each line has been highlighted. Write the correct spelling for each highlighted word in the box.

Menu

14 fried **rise**

15 **butta** chicken

16 **ster**-fried vegetables

17 **cokonut** prawns

18 **solt** and pepper prawns

Answers and explanations on page 85

SPELLING

Intermediate level questions

Mini Test 4

The spelling mistakes in these sentences have been highlighted. Write the correct spelling for each highlighted word in the box.

1 It's Mum's berfday today.

2 How meny candles will go on the cake?

3 A big dog chaset a little dog under the house.

4 Our cat likes to clime trees.

5 Dad seys he will cook pancakes.

6 My teacha is Mr Smart.

7 Mum said to do my homwerk before dinner.

8 Kylie had sum sandwiches for lunch.

9 The rotting seaweed stangk on the sand.

10 Dad is writeing an email to Uncle Greg.

The spelling mistakes in these labels have been highlighted. Write the correct spelling for each highlighted word in the box.

11 clok

12 skiping rope

13 row bowt

Read the text *Body parts*. The spelling mistake in each sentence has been highlighted. Write the correct spelling of each highlighted word in the box.

Body parts

14 I have ten fingers and ten tows.

15 I spy with my two eys.

16 I knelt on my nees.

17 My brane is smart.

18 I follow my noes to the chocolate tart.

Answers and explanations on pages 85–86

SPELLING

Intermediate level questions

Mini Test 5

Each line has a word that is incorrect. Write the correct spelling of the word in the box.

1 Amina ate all the strawberries becorse they were so sweet.

2 Andy remembed to learn his spelling.

3 Wade ate an appel and a pear.

4 Gigantic is a werd that means 'big'.

5 Alice scratched her ichy foot.

6 Dad has a new bloo shirt for work.

7 Nan always tells us to choo our food.

8 Matt has soccer on Tuseday.

9 Take the book to the library on Wensday.

10 Julia's concert is on Munday.

The words below are in pairs of opposite. In each pair one word is spelt incorrectly. Write the correct spelling of the word in the box.

11 big smorll

12 day nite

13 kwick slow

Read the text *Where is Yuki?* Each line has a word that is incorrect. Write the correct spelling of the word in the box.

Where is Yuki?

14 The teacher arskt the class

15 if enybody knew where Yuki was.

16 Sumbody said that Yuki was sick.

17 Evrybody misses Yuki.

18 I hope she sees the docta and gets well soon.

Answers and explanations on pages 86–87

SPELLING

Intermediate level questions

Mini Test 6

Each line has a word that is incorrect. Write the correct spelling of the word in the box.

1 Len lost his bus tickit.

2 James had toste and eggs for breakfast.

3 The mother sheep stood with her lam.

4 "Is this yor hat?" asked Sonia.

5 "Wot time is it?" asked Rafiq.

6 We wocht a show about lions.

7 People skreamed on the roller coaster.

8 The lightning struck sudderly.

9 Mum raked the autumn leeves.

10 We lost electrical powah during the storm.

The words below are in pairs of opposites. In each pair one word is spelt incorrectly. Write the correct spelling of the word in the box.

11 lowd quiet

12 frend enemy

13 babee parent

Read the text *New neighbours*. Each line has a word that is incorrect. Write the correct spelling of the word in the box.

New neighbours

14 A family has bought the howse next door to me.

15 They r moving in

16 on Satday.

17 The house has a larje vegetable garden.

18 I hope they will share their tomartoes.

SPELLING

Advanced level questions

Mini Test 7

The spelling mistakes in these sentences have been highlighted. Write the correct spelling for each highlighted word in the box.

1 Chocolate is the best ise -cream flavour.

2 My dog is happyest when she is digging a hole.

3 The teacher said we were making too much noiz .

4 Children and perents came to Open Day.

5 Some peeple don't eat meat.

6 I can eat dozens of strawberrys .

7 Lily made three wishez and blew out her candles.

8 My dog is in trubble for chewing the chair legs.

9 The teacher said I was useing my brain.

10 A rektangle has four sides.

There is one spelling mistake in each sentence. Shade the bubble under the spelling mistake.

11 Dad carried my sister on his sholders.

12 Mum said I cood play at Ari's house after school.

13 The washing mashine has broken down again.

Read the text *Dad's best dish*. The spelling mistake in each line has been highlighted. Write the correct spelling for each highlighted word in the box.

Dad's best dish

14 Dad has a recipy for

15 cheesy potatos

16 with cream and unions.

17 We eat it so farst

18 we bern our mouths.

Answers and explanations on pages 87–88

SPELLING

Advanced level questions

Mini Test 8

The spelling mistakes in these sentences have been highlighted. Write the correct spelling for each highlighted word in the box.

1 Louella went to the shop with her bruther.

2 Max useally helps with the shopping.

3 Annie ate the hole mango.

4 My next-door nayber lets me eat his mulberries.

5 Neether Mum nor Dad can come to the meeting.

6 The baby larft at the funny dog.

7 We went to the zoo yesstaday.

8 I herd a noise under the house.

9 Only wimmen can play on the team.

10 Wear did you hide the gifts?

There is one spelling mistake in each sentence. Shade the bubble under the spelling mistake.

11 Dad sqirted me with water from the hose.

12 We walked so far my feet hert badly.

13 The teacher said that the persen with the best answer was me.

Read the text *At the zoo*. The spelling mistake in each line has been highlighted. Write the correct spelling for each highlighted word in the box.

At the zoo

14 Last Thirsday we went to the zoo.

15 My favrit animal was

16 the monkee .

17 There were yung ones and old ones.

18 The mothers caird for their babies.

Answers and explanations on pages 88–89

SPELLING Advanced level questions

Mini Test 9

Each line has a word that is incorrect. Write the correct spelling of the word in the box.

1 My little brother hugd me.

2 Mario tried to cach yabbies in the dam.

3 My running shoos are too small now.

4 Zac came forth in the race.

5 Helen tryed to teach me how to skip.

6 John's house is the ateth in the street.

7 Jade cryed in the sad movie.

8 Charlie thought his mother had forgotin him.

9 Sam came nineth in the contest.

The words below are in pairs of opposites. In each pair one word is spelt incorrectly. Write the correct spelling of the word in the box.

10	wellcome	unwelcome
11	possible	immpossible
12	responsible	irrusponsible
13	hopless	hopeful

Read the text *Lunch*. Each line has a word that is incorrect. Write the correct spelling of the word in the box.

Lunch

14 Ella chopped pineapple for the froot salad

15 while Luca cooked pumpkin soop.

16 Their friends were comeing at 12 o'clock

17 which was in thirty minits.

18 They needed to hurri.

Answers and explanations on pages 89–90

Mini Test 10

20 MIN

Each line has a word that is incorrect. Write the correct spelling of the word in the box.

1 Three kittens are feemails and two are males.

2 We walked past a boy playing the gitar.

3 Mum said were going to the beach on Sunday.

4 Dad cooked prorns for my birthday.

5 Melita drew a bewtiful picture.

6 The wooly mammoth is an extinct animal.

7 Today is speshal because it's my birthday.

8 Kali knew all the ansers in the test.

9 The teacher told George to play nisely.

The words below are in pairs. In each pair one word is spelt incorrectly. Write the correct spelling of the word in the box.

10 wolf wolfs

11 bus busses

12 piece peeses

Read the text *A good read*. Each line has a word that is incorrect. Write the correct spelling of the word in the box.

A good read

13 I am reading a scairy story.

14 The auther is Australian.

15 I like to feel fritened in stories.

16 It's great when stories are exsiting.

17 I wurry about what will happen to the characters

18 but I no everyone will be safe in the end.

Answers and explanations on page 90

Mini Test 1

10 MIN

1 Which word correctly completes this sentence?
Mum took ______ to see the dentist.
A we **B** me
C she **D** he

2 Which word correctly completes this sentence?
______ dentist is really nice.
A Its **B** An
C It **D** The

3 Which word correctly completes this sentence?
I ______ to the park.
A ran **B** running **C** runs **D** runner

4 Which word can be used instead of the highlighted words in this sentence?
The dog was thirsty so I gave **the dog** some water.
A she **B** I **C** me **D** it

5 Which word correctly completes this sentence?
An apple is ______ the table.
A before **B** on **C** in **D** along

6 Which word in this sentence describes the dog?
I saw a black dog.
A dog **B** black **C** saw **D** I

7 Which word in this sentence is a noun?
The apple was crunchy.
A The **B** apple **C** was **D** crunchy

8 Which word in this sentence is used to describe the cat?
The lazy cat slept on a chair in the sun.
A sun **B** chair **C** slept **D** lazy

9 Which one of these is a sentence?
A Over the moon. **B** The dish and spoon.
C The cow jumped. **D** Singing happily.

Answers and explanations on pages 90–91

The text below has some words missing. Choose the correct word to complete each sentence.

Bees ______ insects. They have

	were	is	are	was
10	A	B	C	D

two pairs ______ wings.

	of	on	under	between
11	A	B	C	D

Bees ______ honey.

	make	are	to	eat
12	A	B	C	D

13 Which of the following sentences is a question? Write the question mark in the box.

A Feed the cat ☐
B The cat is hungry ☐
C Is the cat hungry ☐
D Look at the cat ☐

14 Which word in this sentence tells **how** an action is done?

You can talk quietly in your groups.

A talk **B** can **C** groups **D** quietly

15 Which sentence is correct?

A Mum and I is growing carrots.
B Mum and I are growing carrots.
C Me and Mum are growing carrots.
D Me and Mum is growing carrots.

16 Which of these words is a plural word (meaning more than one)?

A men **B** woman **C** child **D** parent

17 Which sentence is a command?

A We are cutting out triangles.
B A triangle has three sides.
C Be careful with the scissors.
D The scissors are very sharp.

18 Which word with a similar meaning can replace the highlighted word in this sentence?

The puppy looked so small.

A sleepy **B** dog **C** pretty **D** little

Answers and explanations on pages 90–91

GRAMMAR Intermediate level questions

Mini Test 2

1 Which word correctly completes this sentence?
Our cat hurt his foot so Mum took ______ to the vet.
A her **B** him
C his **D** he

2 Which word in this sentence is a noun?
Be gentle with the cat.
A Be **B** gentle
C with **D** cat

3 Which word correctly completes this sentence?
A flock of cockatoos ______ overhead.
A flying **B** flew **C** flight **D** noisily

4 Which pronoun can be used instead of the highlighted words in this sentence?
Dad and I played in the park.
A We **B** Us **C** Them **D** They

5 Which word correctly completes this sentence?
"Follow me, ducklings," ______ Mother Duck.
A told **B** spoke **C** quacking **D** said

6 Which word in this sentence tells how the children worked?
The children worked quickly.
A children **B** worked **C** The **D** quickly

7 Choose a word to correctly complete the sentence.
Jamilla saw a ______ at the zoo.
A eagle **B** orangutan **C** monkey **D** elephant

8 Which word in this sentence is used to describe the cake?
The delicious cake was baked this morning.
A morning **B** The **C** cake **D** delicious

9 Which one of these is a sentence?
A The hungry little rabbit. **B** Ran swiftly.
C Through the vegetable patch. **D** It was looking for the carrots.

Answers and explanations on page 91

Mini Test 2 (continued)

The text below has some words missing. Choose the correct word or words to complete the text.

		me	I	them	they
Dad and ______ washed the car	10	A	B	C	D
		look	looking	looked	were look
yesterday. It ______ really nice	11	A	B	C	D
		then	while	so	when
______ we had finished.	12	A	B	C	D

13 Which of the following sentences is a question? Write the question mark in the box.

A Don't step on the bee ☐

B It's collecting pollen in the clover ☐

C Can you see the bee ☐

D Let's watch it for a while ☐

14 Which word in this sentence tells **how** to wash your hands?

Wash your hands properly before eating.

A hands **B** properly **C** wash **D** before

15 Which sentence is correct?

A Ben and me are in the soccer team. **B** Ben and I is in the soccer team.

C Ben and I are in the soccer team. **D** Ben and me is in the soccer team.

16 Which word correctly completes this sentence?

Ben ______ the ball between the goalposts.

A kicking **B** kicker **C** kick **D** kicked

17 Which sentence is **not** a command?

A Kick the ball to Daniella. **B** Daniella is a good player.

C Get the ball, Daniella. **D** Tie your shoelaces.

18 Which word with a similar meaning can replace the highlighted word in this sentence?

The game was very exciting.

A quiet **B** silly **C** thrilling **D** dull

Answers and explanations on page 91

GRAMMAR
Intermediate level questions

Mini Test 3

1 Which word correctly completes this sentence?
We sat ______ the umbrella.
A in B above
C over D under

2 Which word correctly completes this sentence?
Dad is taking ______ to collect my new uniform.
A myself B she
C me D he

3 Which word or words correctly complete this sentence?
Kelly ______ porridge for breakfast this morning.
A having B had C were having D have

4 Which pronoun can be used instead of *Ryan and Lara* in this sentence?
Ryan and Lara are playing outside.
A We B Them C Ourselves D They

5 Which word correctly completes this sentence?
It was hot ______ the children decided to go for a swim.
A but B although C because D so

6 Which word in this sentence is an action verb?
Paula caught the ball with one hand.
A caught B ball C Paula D one

7 In which sentence is there a mistake?
A Our teacher read us a poem.
B It was about a thunderstorm.
C It made the storm sound loud and scary.
D I could heard the rain and thunder.

8 Which word in this sentence is used to describe the storm?
A wild storm swept through the city.
A wild B storm C swept D through

9 Which of the following is a sentence?
A The thunder was loud. B The lightning.
C Flashes in the sky. D Bright in the night.

Answers and explanations on pages 91–92

Mini Test 3 (continued)

The text below has some words missing. Choose the correct word to complete each sentence.

		A	B	C	D
Gia ______ swimming lessons every	10	is	done	gone	has
Tuesday. Her best stroke ______ free	11	has	is	have	are
style. She likes swimming very ______.	12	much	most	really	many

13 Which of these sentences is a command?

A Wear a bike helmet.

B A helmet protects your head.

C Helmets are sometimes called 'stack hats'.

D You do not want to 'stack' your bike.

14 Which word in this sentence tells **how** to pat the kitten?

Pat the tiny kitten gently.

A Pat B tiny C kitten D gently

15 Which word correctly completes this sentence?

Dad said not to use too ______ glue.

A many B most C more D much

16 Which word correctly completes this sentence?

Mum said, "Here's your glass. Don't drop ______."

A her B him C it D them

17 Which word correctly completes this text?

Wombats have sharp claws. ______ dig burrows.

A They B Them C She D It

18 Which word in this sentence is a noun?

She ate her lunch slowly.

A She B ate C lunch D slowly

Answers and explanations on pages 91–92

GRAMMAR Advanced level questions

Mini Test 4

20 MIN

1 Which word in this sentence is a noun?
The bird chirped loudly.
A The B bird
C chirped D loudly

2 Which word correctly completes this sentence?
I asked my nanna to make ______ a cake.
A myself B she
C me D her

3 Which word or words correctly complete this sentence?
We ______ noodles for dinner last night.
A cooked B cooking C was cooked D cooks

4 Which pronoun correctly completes this sentence?
Luis and Mario said, "Come with ______ to the museum."
A we B them C ourselves D us

5 Which word correctly completes this sentence?
I'm eating an apple ______ I'm hungry.
A but B then C because D so

6 Which word in this sentence is an action verb?
Hugo chewed a gigantic bone.
A bone B gigantic C Hugo D chewed

7 In which sentence is there a mistake?
A I saw a gecko on the wall.
B It was chasing a cockroach.
C The cockroach run away quickly.
D The gecko called, "Chuck, chuck, chuck."

8 Which word in this sentence is used as an adjective?
The sneaky gecko watched the cockroach.
A sneaky B gecko C watched D cockroach

9 Which of the following is a sentence?
A On the wall. B In the kitchen.
C There was a spider. D A big brown spider.

Answers and explanations on page 92

Mini Test 4 (continued)

The text below has some words missing. Choose the correct word to complete each sentence.

Last Saturday, I ______ to the national

	went	come	gone	go
10	A	B	C	D

park with my family. ______ went

	They	Us	We	He
11	A	B	C	D

bushwalking. I had lots ______ fun.

	with	in	for	of
12	A	B	C	D

13 Which of these sentences is a command?

A Do your homework.
B Would you like to help?
C I can help you do your homework.
D I have spelling homework.

14 Which word in this sentence tells **how** to stir the hot soup?

Stir the hot soup carefully.

A stir B soup C hot D carefully

15 Which sentence is correct?

A Mum and I like to surf.
B Mum and me like to surf.
C Me and mum like to surf.
D Us like to surf.

16 Which of these words **cannot** be used as a plural (to mean more than one)?

A fish B sheep C mice D cow

17 Which sentence can be completed correctly with *where*?

A We ______ in a hurry?
B ______ you late for class?
C ______ are you going?
D Why ______ you late for class?

18 Which word correctly completes this sentence?

We built ______ sandcastle at the beach.

A those B an C some D a

Answers and explanations on page 92

GRAMMAR Advanced level questions

Mini Test 5

1 Which word in this sentence is a noun?

I went to the library.

A I B went
C the D library

2 Which word or words correctly complete this sentence?

The children ______ their lunches under a tree.

A did ate B eating
C are eating D is eating

3 Which word correctly completes this sentence?

Kim sat on the bench ______ she could eat her lunch.

A after B when C that D so

4 Which word correctly completes this sentence?

I've been waiting a long time ______ Mum is running late.

A until B then C because D why

5 Which word in this sentence is an action verb?

The crocodile snapped its strong jaws.

A jaws B crocodile C snapped D strong

6 In which sentence is there a mistake?

A A huntsman spider stands in the corner.
B It waits for dinner to strolled by.
C It is patient.
D I think it waits for a cockroach.

7 Which word in this sentence is used as an adjective?

The huntsman is a large spider.

A huntsman B large C spider D The

8 Which of the following is a sentence?

A Saltwater crocodiles will.
B Attack humans who enter their territory.
C Adult saltwater crocodiles will eat anything.
D Even sharks.

9 Which word in this sentence tells **how** to mix eggs and flour?

Slowly mix the eggs and the flour.

A slowly B mix C egg D and

Answers and explanations on pages 92–93

Mini Test 5 (continued)

The text below has some words missing. Choose the correct word or words to complete each sentence.

The blue-ringed octopus ______ in rock

10 A lived B lives C living D live

pools at the seaside. It hides ______ rocks

11 A under B over C through D beside

and shells. It ______ eight arms. Its rings

12 A have B had C has D is

turn bright blue ______ it

13 A then B however C although D when

is angry. ______ is poisonous.

14 A That B They C It D He

15 Which pronoun correctly completes this sentence?

Paco and Emily decided to go to the park. I went with ______.

A they B her C you D them

16 Which word correctly completes this sentence?

The flock of geese ______ flying north.

A were B are C is D gone

17 Which sentence can be completed correctly with *were*?

A ______ is my hat?

B Why ______ you late?

C ______ going to the beach on the weekend.

D ______ are you going?

18 Which word correctly completes this sentence?

The children finished ______ work quickly.

A their B there C they're D there's

Answers and explanations on pages 92–93

PUNCTUATION Standard level questions

Mini Test 1

10 MIN

1 Which sentence has the correct punctuation at the end?

A We love reading?
B We love reading.
C We love reading
D We love reading,

2 Which sentence is punctuated correctly?

A I like ella.
B I like ella?
C I like Ella
D I like Ella.

3 Which sentence is punctuated correctly?

A Mum went to China
B Mum went to China.
C mum went to China
D mum went to China.

4 Which sentence is punctuated correctly?

A please feed the cat
B please feed the cat.
C please feed the cat?
D Please feed the cat.

5 Which word should start with a capital letter?

A boy
B child
C james
D children

6 Which sentence is punctuated correctly?

A I live in Cooma.
B I live in cooma.
C I live in Cooma
D i live in cooma

7 Which word should start with a capital letter?

A place
B australia
C beach
D city

8 Which word needs a capital letter? *My friend's name is milly.*

A friend's
B name
C is
D milly

9 A full stop (.) is missing from this sentence.
Where does the missing full stop go?

We had (A) pasta (B) with prawns (C) for dinner (D)

10 Which of the following correctly completes the sentence?

Do you have a ______

A pencil?
B pencil.
C pencil!
D Pencil.

Answers and explanations on page 93

11 Which punctuation correctly completes the sentence?
"Run ____" shouted Harley.

A ! **B** , **C** ? **D** .

12 Which punctuation correctly completes the sentence?
Bill walks to school ____

A ! **B** ? **C** , **D** .

13 Which word should start with a capital letter?
I have a brother named greg.

A named **B** greg **C** have **D** brother

14 Which punctuation correctly completes the sentence?
How old are you ____

A ? **B** . **C** ! **D** ,

15 Which word should start with a capital letter?
I would like to go to africa to see elephants.

A would **B** africa **C** elephants **D** see

16 Which sentence is punctuated correctly?

A My Birthday is in February.
B My birthday is in february.
C My birthday is in February
D My birthday is in February.

17 Which sentence has the correct punctuation at the end?

A Bella played with her cat
B Bella played with her cat.
C Bella played with her cat,
D Bella played with her cat?

18 Which sentence is punctuated correctly?

A We went to the beach on Sunday?
B We went to the beach on Sunday.
C We went to the beach on Sunday
D We went to the beach on Sunday,

Answers and explanations on page 93

PUNCTUATION Intermediate level questions

Mini Test 2

18 MIN

1 Which sentence is punctuated correctly?

A Holly has a new baby brother,
B Holly has a new baby brother.
C Holly has a new baby brother
D Holly has a new baby brother?

2 Which sentence is punctuated correctly?

A My 'teacher' is really funny,
B My Teacher is really funny?
C My teacher is really funny.
D My Teacher is really funny!

3 Which sentence is punctuated correctly?

A José wants to play cricket.
B josé wants to play cricket
C josé wants to play cricket?
D José wants, to play, cricket!

4 Which sentence is punctuated correctly?

A Dad asked me to help with the dishes.
B Dad asked me to help with the dishes?
C Dad asked me to help with the dishes
D dad asked me to help with the dishes.

5 Which punctuation correctly completes the sentence?

Hamish has soccer after school today

A !   **B** ,   **C** ?   **D** .

6 Which sentence is punctuated correctly?

A I have swimming on Mondays.
B I have swimming on mondays.
C I have swimming on Mondays
D I have Swimming on Mondays!

7 Which punctuation correctly completes the text?

Ned caught a bus to Bondi

A ?   **B** ,   **C** .   **D** !

8 Which word can replace *I am* in this sentence?

I am hungry.

A I'am   **B** I'm   **C** Im'   **D** Iam'

Answers and explanations on pages 93–94

9 A comma is missing from this sentence. Where does the missing comma go?

Let's take (A) Scruff (B) Bluey (C) and (D) Dino to the creek.

10 Which of the following correctly completes the sentence?

Have you finished your ______

A work? **B** work. **C** work! **D** Work?

11 Which punctuation correctly completes the sentence?

"Stop ______ " shouted Becca.

A . **B** , **C** ? **D** !

12 Which of the following correctly completes the sentence?

What's the time ______

A . **B** ! **C** , **D** ?

13 Which word should start with a capital letter?

We are going camping in the december school holidays.

A camping **B** december **C** school **D** holidays

14 Which sentence correctly uses the question mark?

A Where is the dog? **B** It's time for dinner?
C The dog ate its dinner? **D** The cat is chasing the dog?

15 Which sentence is punctuated correctly?

A Dan asked if today was Tuesday. **B** dan asked if today was Tuesday
C Dan asked if today was Tuesday? **D** Dan asked if today was tuesday.

16 Which sentence is punctuated correctly?

A Arthur's birthday is in february. **B** Arthur's Birthday is in February,
C Arthur's birthday is in February. **D** Arthur's birthday is in february!

17 Which of the following correctly completes the sentence?

ANZAC Day is in ______

A april. **B** April. **C** april? **D** April

18 Which of the following correctly completes the sentence?

Mum added ______ to the shopping list.

A milk, cream, and shampoo, **B** milk, cream and, shampoo
C milk, cream and shampoo **D** milk, cream, and shampoo

Answers and explanations on pages 93–94

PUNCTUATION Intermediate level questions

Mini Test 3

18 MIN

1 Which sentence is punctuated correctly?

A the teacher read to the class
B The teacher read to the class.
C The Teacher, read to the class,
D The teacher read to the class?

2 Which punctuation correctly completes the sentence?

My teacher's name is Ms Fong ______
A ! **B** ,
C . **D** ?

3 Which punctuation correctly completes the sentence?
"HELP ______ " screamed Mary.
A . **B** , **C** ! **D** ?

4 Which sentence is punctuated correctly?

A Nana asked us to help her with the garden?
B Nana asked us to help her with the garden.
C Nana, asked us, to help her, with the garden.
D Nana asked us to help her with the garden

5 Which sentence is punctuated correctly?
A Mum said to buy bread, milk, bananas and honey
B Mum said to buy bread, milk, bananas and honey.
C Mum said to buy bread milk bananas and honey
D Mum said to buy bread, milk, bananas, and honey.

6 Which sentence is punctuated correctly?
A olivia lives at 8 Rose street, Belrose. **B** Olivia lives at 8 rose street, belrose.
C Olivia lives at 8 Rose Street, Belrose. **D** Olivia lives at 8 Rose Street, Belrose

7 A full stop is missing from this sentence. Where does the missing full stop go?
I (A) went (B) to Westdale (C) Shopping Village (D)

8 There are two sentences here. Where does the missing full stop go?
I wear (A) a hat (B) when I play outdoors (C) I won't (D) get sunburnt.

Answers and explanations on pages 94–95

9 A comma is missing from this sentence. Where does the missing comma go?

First of all (A) we need to add (B) the flour (C) eggs (D) and sugar.

10 Which of the following correctly completes the sentence?

What time do you start ______

A school? B school. C school! D School,

11 Which punctuation correctly completes the text?

Stephen called, "Wait ______ "

A ! B , C ? D ,

12 Which of the following correctly completes the sentence?

Do you know what time the movie ______

A starts. B starts! C starts? D starts,

13 Which word should start with a capital letter?

I live in canberra with my mother, father and brother.

A canberra B mother C father D brother

14 Which sentence uses the question mark correctly?

A Is he a good dog?
B Jasmine loves to make cakes?
C Kyle had to tie his shoelaces?
D Wait for me?

15 Which sentence is punctuated correctly?

A Where did you see the bear.
B where did You see the bear?
C where did you see the bear!
D Where did you see the bear?

16 Which sentence is punctuated correctly?

A Sunil is ten years old
B sunil is ten years old
C Sunil is ten years old.
D Sunil is Ten years old.

17 Which of the following correctly completes the sentence?

Australia Day is in ______

A January. B january. C January? D January

18 A full stop is missing from this text. Where does the missing full stop go?

We slept (A) in tents (B) Our sleeping bags (C) were snug (D) and warm.

Answers and explanations on pages 94–95

PUNCTUATION Advanced level questions

Mini Test 4

20 MIN

1 Which sentence is punctuated correctly?
A julie vivas illustrates children's books.
B Julie Vivas illustrates children's books.
C Julie Vivas illustrates children's books
D Julie vivas illustrates children's books.

2 Which sentence is punctuated correctly?
A *Wilfrid Gordon McDonald Partridge* is a lovely book.
B *Wilfrid Gordon McDonald Partridge* is a lovely book
C *Wilfrid gordon McDonald partridge* is a lovely book?
D *Wilfrid gordon McDonald partridge* is a lovely book,

3 Which sentence is punctuated correctly?
A We have art on wednesday.
B we have art on Wednesday.
C We have art on wednesday.
D We have art on Wednesday.

4 Which sentence is punctuated correctly?
A Mum said that I had to clean the fish tank?
B Mum said that "I had to clean the fish tank."
C Mum said that I had to clean the fish tank.
D Mum said that I had to clean the fish tank?

5 Which sentence is punctuated correctly?
A Dad said to tidy my room, make my bed and help with dinner.
B Dad said to tidy my room make my bed and help with dinner.
C Dad said to "tidy my room, make my bed and help with dinner."
D Dad said "to tidy my room, make my bed and help with dinner."

6 Which sentence is punctuated correctly?
A katie lives in victoria
B Katie lives in Victoria.
C Katie lives in victoria.
D Katie lives in Victoria

7 A full stop is missing. Where does the missing full stop go?

Peter, James and Chloe (A) go to the same school (B) They catch the bus (C) each (D) morning.

8 Which sentence uses the exclamation mark (**!**) correctly?
A I love it!
B Do you really like my new pencil case!
C What's the time!
D Where did you get that pencil case!

Answers and explanations on page 95

Mini Test 4 (continued)

9 A comma is missing from this sentence. Where does the missing comma go?

I like to eat (A) strawberries (B) raspberries (C) and yoghurt (D) for breakfast.

10 Which of the following correctly completes the sentence?

Will you be able to finish your homework before ______

A dinner? **B** dinner! **C** dinner. **D** Dinner?

11 Which of the following correctly completes the sentence?

Daniel shouted, "Don't go in there ______

A !" **B** " **C** ?" **D** ,"

12 Which of the following correctly completes the sentence?

Dad asked what I wanted for ______

A Dinner. **B** dinner. **C** dinner?" **D** dinner!

13 Which word should start with a capital letter?

I helped (A) sally with (B) our (C) punctuation homework yesterday (D) afternoon.

14 Which sentence correctly uses the question mark?

A There's a worm in my apple? **B** Why were you late?

C School starts at 9 am? **D** It's 10 am?

15 Which sentence is correctly punctuated?

A boris and natalie were married in june

B boris and natalie were married in June.

C Boris and Natalie were married in June.

D Boris and Natalie were married in june?

16 Which sentence is correctly punctuated?

A We are having a holiday with our friends in Sydney

B we are having a holiday with our friends in Sydney

C we are having a holiday with our friends in sydney

D We are having a holiday with our friends in Sydney.

17 Which of the following correctly completes the sentence?

The book was called ______.

A *treasure island* **B** *Treasure island* **C** *Treasure Island.* **D** *Treasure island?*

18 Which punctuation correctly completes the sentence?

"Who left a mess on the floor ______" asked Dan.

A ? **B** ! **C** , **D** .

Answers and explanations on page 95

PUNCTUATION Advanced level questions

Mini Test 5

1 Which sentence is punctuated correctly?
A My favourite author is paul jennings.
B My favourite author is Paul Jennings
C My favourite author is Paul Jennings.
D My favourite Author is paul Jennings.

2 Which sentence is punctuated correctly?
A My friend Jack likes reading stories about dogs,
B My friend jack likes reading stories about Dogs
C My friend Jack likes reading stories about dogs
D My friend Jack likes reading stories about dogs.

3 Which sentence is punctuated correctly?
A Does Christine like funny stories best?
B Does Christine like funny stories best!
C Does Christine like funny stories best.
D Does christine like funny stories best?

4 Which sentence is punctuated correctly?
A my cat's name is Moustache, which is French for whiskers.
B My cat's name is moustache, which is French for whiskers.
C My cat's name is Moustache, which is French for whiskers.
D My cat's name is moustache, which is French for whiskers.

5 Which sentence is punctuated correctly?
A dad is getting a haircut on Monday.
B Dad is getting a haircut on monday.
C Dad is getting a haircut on Monday
D Dad is getting a haircut on Monday.

6 Which sentence is punctuated correctly?
A Indira was born in India.
B Indira was born in India
C Indira was born in india.
D indira was born in india

7 Which word is missing a capital letter?
Kiki takes her dog to the same park as me. we go there after school.
A dog B park C we D school

8 Which of the following correctly completes the sentence?
"Is that peach ______ " asked Gina.
A juicy? B juicy! C juicy. D juicy,

Answers and explanations on pages 95–96

9 A comma is missing from the sentence. Where does the missing comma go?

Mum (A) made beef patties (B) with mince (C) onion (D) and an egg.

10 Which of the following correctly completes the sentence?

Do you agree with Tina's ______

A opinion? B opinion! C opinion. D Opinion?

11 Which punctuation correctly completes the text?

Kerry whispered, "This movie is really funny ______

A !" B " C ?" D ."

12 Which of the following correctly completes the sentence?

Dad told us to make our own ______

A Sandwiches. B sandwiches. C sandwiches?" D sandwiches?

13 Which word should start with a capital letter?

The (A) children worked (B) together to finish the (C) mural last (D) sunday.

14 A full stop is missing from this text. Where does the missing full stop go?

I went (A) to the shop (B) Todd (C) came (D) too.

15 Which sentence is correctly punctuated?

A It's cold in the mountains in July B It's cold in the mountains in july
C Its cold in the Mountains in july. D It's cold in the mountains in July.

16 Which punctuation correctly completes the sentence?

When will we see Uncle Ron ______

A ! B ? C . D ,"

17 A full stop is missing from this text. Where does the missing full stop go?

Harry read (A) a book (B) called (C) *The Little Refugee* (D) I read it too.

18 Which of the following correctly completes the sentence?

I had ______ on my sandwich.

A cheese, tomato and lettuce B a cheese, tomato, and lettuce
C a cheese tomato and lettuce. D a cheese, tomato, and lettuce,

Answers and explanations on pages 95–96

READING Standard level questions

Mini Test 1: Poster

A poster:
- tries to get your attention
- might use big letters, bright colours and photos.

Read the poster *Lost dog* and answer the questions. Circle the correct answers.

1. What is the lost dog's name?
   A Jack
   B Bluebird
   C Scooter
   D Mary

2. Who owns the lost dog?
   A a boy
   B a girl
   C Lulu
   D a family

3. What does the lost dog do on command?
   A sits
   B jumps
   C barks
   D eats

4. Draw lines to connect the adjectives to the correct nouns from the text.

white	collar
short	dog
tan	hair
blue	ears

5. How do you think the dog's owners feel?
   A angry **B** sad **C** surprised **D** tired

6. What is the purpose of the poster?
   A to help you choose a pet dog
   B to help find a lost dog
   C to advertise a dog for sale
   D to explain about dogs

Answers and explanations on pages 96–97

Mini Test 2: Advertisement

An advertisement:
- is a persuasive text
- tries to get you to buy something or do something.

Read the advertisement *New! Blue Chompees* and answer the questions. Circle the correct answers.

1. What is a Blue Chompee?
   A a sweet treat
   B a healthy snack
   C an ice block
   D a toy

2. This advertisement wants you to
   A do cartwheels.
   B share things with friends.
   C buy Blue Chompees.
   D watch more TV.

3. Why does the advertisement want you to *Have some every day*?
   A so you have more energy
   B so you buy more
   C so you have more fun
   D so you have some to share with others

4. **Who** does the advertisement say Blue Chompees are for?
   A only schoolchildren
   B family and friends
   C children
   D just you

5. You can get Blue Chompees from
   A school.
   B your parents.
   C teachers.
   D shops.

6. Choose two answers. Blue Chompees are probably
   A purple.
   B green.
   C blue.
   D red.
   E healthy.
   F unhealthy.

Answers and explanations on page 97

READING

Intermediate level questions

Mini Test 3: Recount

A recount:
- is an informative text
- tells about events that have happened.

Read the recount *Joey* and answer the questions. Circle the correct answers.

Joey

My aunt looks after native animals that have been hurt. A while ago she was given a little joey to look after. The mother kangaroo had been killed by a car. Someone found the joey alive in the mother's pouch. They took it to a wildlife sanctuary.

At the sanctuary hospital a vet took some X-rays. Luckily the joey had no broken bones so it didn't have to stay in hospital. My aunt took the joey to her home. She had to feed it every four hours, day and night, for the first few weeks. She gave it bottles of formula. It was so cute. It slept inside a baby's blanket that my aunt had made into a pouch.

When the joey was able to look after itself it went to live in a paddock at the sanctuary with other kangaroos. Maybe one day soon it can go back into the wild.

1. The vet checked the joey for
   A broken bones. **B** X-rays. **C** ticks. **D** friendliness.

2. The joey's mother had been killed
   A by a fox. **B** by its mother. **C** by the aunt. **D** by a car.

3. The writer's aunt
   A is a school teacher. **B** feeds kangaroos.
   C looks after animals that are hurt. **D** works in a zoo.

4. The joey needed feeding
   A every four hours. **B** for a long time.
   C until it could drink water. **D** all day.

5. The joey now lives
   A with the writer's aunt. **B** in the wildlife sanctuary.
   C in a zoo. **D** in the wild.

6. Where did the joey sleep at the aunt's home?
   A with the dog **B** in a backpack **C** in bed **D** in a blanket

Answers and explanations on page 97

READING

Intermediate level questions

Mini Test 4: Discussion

A discussion:

- shares differing ideas about a topic.

Read the discussion *Flightless birds* and answer the questions. Circle the correct answers.

Flightless birds

Year 3 is talking about birds that can't fly.

Becca: Emus and ostriches can't fly. Their wings are too small and they are too heavy.

Paul: Cassowaries are like emus. They can't fly either.

Josh: What's a cassowary?

Teacher: It's a large flightless bird that lives in the rainforests of North Queensland. The rhea from South America can't fly either.

Arnold: Kiwis can't fly.

Tia: Kiwis are from New Zealand. I saw some in a zoo when I went to visit my grandparents. Kiwis are the size of chickens. Their wings are just way too tiny so they can't fly.

Teacher: Yes, that's right. Sometimes kiwis get killed by cats, dogs, ferrets and cars because they can't fly away. The dodo is an extinct flightless bird. Has anyone heard of the dodo? Dodos became extinct because they couldn't fly away from hunters.

Josh: My nana laughs and calls me a dodo when I'm being silly.

Becca: What about penguins? They don't fly. Wow! There's lots of birds that can't fly.

1. How many flightless birds did the class discuss?
   - **A** 5
   - **B** 1
   - **C** 7
   - **D** 4

2. Cassowaries can't fly because
   - **A** they look like emus.
   - **B** they have long legs to run out of harm's way.
   - **C** they don't have any wings.
   - **D** their wings are too small.

3. When Josh's nana calls him a dodo
   - **A** she is being mean.
   - **B** she is making a joke.
   - **C** she thinks he eats too much chicken.
   - **D** she knows he cannot fly.

4. Which animal or animals kill kiwis?
   - **A** cassowaries
   - **B** cats, dogs, ferrets and cars
   - **C** cats, dogs and ferrets
   - **D** other New Zealand animals

5. Where do rheas live?
   - **A** South America
   - **B** North Queensland
   - **C** New Zealand
   - **D** where cassowaries live

6. The class is talking about flightless birds
   - **A** to learn how to fly.
   - **B** to practise for a test about emus.
   - **C** to share ideas.
   - **D** to learn about other countries.

Answers and explanations on page 97

READING

Intermediate level questions

Mini Test 5: Poem

A poem:

- entertains
- can describe something, give an opinion or tell a story
- might use rhyme, or sounds and word patterns.

Read the poem *Crocodile* and answer the questions. Circle the correct answers.

Crocodile

On the river
one day
I saw a crocodile.
It came floating by;
a log with yellow eyes.
It did not blink.
It simply drifted,
silently.

Along the river
I saw a crocodile
on a sandbank,
baking in the sun.
It did not blink.
It simply watched
as I drifted by,
silently.

Tricky things
those crocodiles.
They seem
so still and quiet.
But …
don't be fooled!
Don't think they're gentle.
Don't think they're friendly.

They can move quickly.
One swish of a tail
and
one snap of the jaws
and
crunch!
There's no escaping
a crocodile.

1. The crocodile makes this noise when it bites something.
   A gulp **B** crunch
   C swish **D** quiet

2. The crocodile looks
   A like a river. **B** like a log.
   C quiet. **D** like a boat.

3. What did the crocodile do on the sandbank?
   A snapped its jaws **B** sunbaked
   C blinked **D** drifted by

4. What warning does the poet give about crocodiles?
   A They eat fish.
   B They don't blink.
   C Don't be fooled.
   D Be still and quiet.

5. What does the poet think of crocodiles?
   A They are sleepy.
   B They are logs.
   C They are still and quiet.
   D They are tricky.

6. Which sentence is true in the poem?
   A Crocodiles are friendly.
   B Crocodiles are gentle.
   C Crocodiles can move quickly.
   D Crocodiles lie on logs.

Answers and explanations on page 98

READING

Intermediate level questions

Mini Test 6: Narrative

8 MIN

A narrative:
- tells a story
- entertains
- might also teach readers a lesson about life.

Read the narrative *It's not right* and answer the questions. Circle the correct answers.

It's not right

Luca was shocked when he saw Lisa put the chocolate bar in her pocket and walk out of the shop. She didn't pay for it!

He quickly ran after her. She was walking away down the street. He caught up. They walked for a few minutes without talking.

Then he said, "I saw what you did."

"So?"

'What if you got caught?" he asked.

"I didn't."

"But you might have," he said.

"But I didn't." She sounded angry with him.

They were quiet for a few minutes.

"I'll share it with you when we get to the park," she offered.

"I don't want any. It's not right." He walked away and went home.

When he got home his mum was in the kitchen chopping vegetables. He sat at the table. He didn't know what to say. He wasn't happy with Lisa. It was wrong to steal things. But he liked Lisa. She was his friend. If he told his mother maybe she could talk with Lisa's mother. He didn't want to get Lisa into trouble but he didn't want her to keep stealing things. She could end up in really big trouble. He decided to tell his mother.

1 How did Luca feel when he saw what Lisa did?
- **A** shocked
- **B** happy
- **C** angry
- **D** sad

2 What had Lisa done?
- **A** spoken angrily to Luca
- **B** walked away from Luca
- **C** stolen something
- **D** eaten a chocolate bar

3 Why doesn't Luca want any chocolate?
- **A** It's unhealthy.
- **B** He doesn't like chocolate.
- **C** He's not hungry.
- **D** Lisa didn't pay for it.

4 What does Luca decide to do in the end?
- **A** help his mother in the kitchen
- **B** not talk to Lisa
- **C** not be friends with Lisa
- **D** tell his mother what Lisa did

5 What do you think Luca will say to his mother?
- **A** Lisa is not my friend any more.
- **B** Lisa stole from a shop.
- **C** I don't like Lisa.
- **D** Is it wrong to steal things?

6 What does Luca hope his mother will do?
- **A** cook a delicious dinner
- **B** talk to Lisa's teacher
- **C** talk to Lisa's mother
- **D** talk to Lisa

Answers and explanations on page 98

READING

Advanced level questions

10 MIN

Mini Test 7: Playscript

A playscript:

- is a narrative that is written for characters to speak or act out.

Read the playscript *She got away* and answer the questions. Circle the correct answers.

She got away

Scene: Papa, Mama and Baby Bear are talking to two police officers.

Mama Bear: We came home from our walk and found that our house had been broken into.

Papa Bear: We found someone asleep in Baby Bear's bed but she escaped.

Baby Bear: (sobbing) She ate my porridge and broke my favourite chair.

Officer 1: How did the intruder get in?

Papa Bear: We think she climbed in through the kitchen window.

Officer 2: Was anything stolen?

Mama Bear: We don't think anything is missing, except Baby's porridge.

Officer 1: When she ran off, in which direction did she travel?

Mama Bear: She ran left down our street and turned right onto Briar Lane. We lost sight of her after that.

Baby Bear: She's a really fast runner.

Officer 2: What did she look like?

Baby Bear: She had long curly yellow hair.

Officer 1: What was she wearing?

Baby Bear: She had on a red hoodie and dark blue pants.

Officer 1: We'll check the porridge bowl, spoon, bed and kitchen window for fingerprints.

Officer 2: And we'll ask people along Briar Lane if they saw a running girl with long curly yellow hair.

Answers and explanations on pages 98–99

Mini Test 7 (continued)

1 What is an *intruder*?

A someone who comes onto your property without permission
B someone who eats your food
C a thief
D someone who runs away from you

2 Where was the intruder when the bears arrived home from their walk?

A in a chair
B eating porridge in the kitchen
C in bed
D running away from the house

3 What does this mean?

… in which direction did she travel?

A Did she travel by herself?
B Which way did she go?
C Did she ask for directions from anyone?
D Did she travel a long way?

4 What does this mean?

We lost sight of her after that.

A The intruder lost her sight.
B The bears didn't see the intruder.
C The intruder disappeared like magic.
D The bears couldn't see her after she turned onto Briar Lane.

5 Choose the best description of the intruder.

A a girl with long curly yellow hair who likes to eat porridge
B a girl wearing a red hoodie and dark blue pants
C a fast runner with yellow hair
D a girl with long curly yellow hair, wearing a red hoodie and dark blue pants

6 Which word tells that Baby Bear was upset?

A broke
B stolen
C sobbing
D favourite

Answers and explanations on pages 98–99

READING **Advanced level questions**

10 MIN

Mini Test 8: Report

A report:

- gives information about a topic.

Read the report *Common paper wasps* and answer the questions. Circle the correct answers or write an answer.

Common paper wasps

Common paper wasps are flying insects. They are very dark brown or black with yellow stripes. They have two pairs of brown wings. They have yellow faces with large eyes.

Common paper wasps are social insects. They live in small colonies. They make nests using chewed-up wood and plant stems, mixed with saliva. They sometimes make their nests on outside walls of people's homes.

The queen wasp lays all the eggs in the nest. Larvae hatch from the eggs. The larvae are fed chewed-up caterpillars and other insects. Larvae grow into pupae. Each pupa is sealed inside its own cell in the nest, where it turns into an adult wasp. When the adult wasp emerges from its cell it becomes a worker in the colony. Adult wasps eat nectar.

Paper wasps are good for gardens. They kill insects such as caterpillars. Caterpillars can destroy gardens. Paper wasps carry pollen from one flower to the next as they feed on plant nectar.

Paper wasps will attack humans who disturb their nest. They have a very painful sting.

Answers and explanations on page 99

Mini Test 8 (continued)

1 Paper wasp nests are made using
A dead caterpillars.
B colonies.
C chewed-up wood and saliva.
D a queen and worker wasps.

2 Write the numbers 1 to 4 in the boxes to show the order of events in the text. The first one [1] has been done for you.

1	The queen lays eggs.
	Adult wasps emerge from cells.
	Larvae grow into pupae stage.
	Larvae hatch from the eggs.

3 Circle true or false.

A Adult paper wasps eat chewed-up insects.	TRUE / FALSE
B Paper wasp larvae hatch from eggs.	TRUE / FALSE
C Adult paper wasps eat nectar.	TRUE / FALSE
D It is good that paper wasps kill caterpillars.	TRUE / FALSE
E It's a bad idea to disturb a paper wasp nest.	TRUE / FALSE

4 The queen wasp lays
A one hundred eggs.
B one egg a day.
C all the eggs.
D enough eggs for dinner.

5 Why should gardeners like paper wasps?
A They kill insects that harm gardens.
B They chew wood.
C They make nests from dead sticks.
D They attack humans.

6 Paper wasps might sting a person
A who kills caterpillars.
B who has a BBQ outdoors.
C who disturbs their nest.
D who they don't like.

Answers and explanations on page 99

READING Advanced level questions

Mini Test 9: Description

A description:

- gives information about a topic
- can be factual, realistic, funny or give opinions.

Read the description *My best friend* and answer the questions. Circle the correct answers.

My best friend

My best friend's name is Sasha. He is really funny. He makes me laugh all the time. Sometimes he can be a bit cheeky in class. Then he gets into trouble. He is really smart at maths and spelling.

Sasha has a wheelchair. He was born with a disability. He can't walk or run but he can use his upper body. He is really good at zooming around in his wheelchair. The rest of us in the class have to be careful not to leave things on the floor in his way. We try to be tidy and considerate. Sometimes we are a bit careless with our bags, especially if we are in a hurry. Then Sasha gets angry with us.

Sasha says one day he is going to compete in the Paralympics. I think he will be awesome. I think he will play wheelchair basketball. He is really good at shooting goals.

I think a best friend is someone you enjoy being with. A best friend makes you feel happy. Sasha is my best friend.

1 How does the writer feel about Sasha?
A enjoys his company
B worries about him
C wishes he was as good as Sasha in maths and spelling
D thinks he should not be cheeky in class

2 Sasha gets into trouble for
A getting annoyed at classmates.
B running over people's things in his wheelchair.
C being cheeky.
D making everyone laugh.

3 Sasha's disability means he can't
A do schoolwork. **B** walk or run.
C play sport. **D** throw a ball.

4 What sport might Sasha play in the Paralympics?
A goal throwing
B zooming around in his wheelchair
C wheelchair races
D basketball

5 What makes Sasha angry?
A being in a wheelchair
B children's bags scattered around the floor
C maths and spelling
D people who can't play basketball

6 The text gives the writer's opinions about
A people with disabilities.
B the Paralympics.
C friendship.
D school.

Answers and explanations on page 99

READING

Advanced level questions

Mini Test 10: Explanation

An explanation:
- tells how or why things happen
- uses technical words.

Read the explanation *Oxygen* and answer the questions. Circle the correct answers or write an answer.

Oxygen

Oxygen is a gas in the air. Humans breathe in oxygen with every breath. The oxygen goes into our lungs. From there it goes into our blood. Then the heart pumps the blood around the body. The blood carries the oxygen out to all our cells and then back to our lungs. When the blood returns to the lungs most of its oxygen is gone.

The heart pumps blood around our bodies constantly, whether we are resting or exercising. However, when we are exercising we need much more oxygen than when we are resting. Our muscles use up oxygen faster when they are working. This makes us breathe faster. We might puff and pant. Puffing, panting and deep breathing help to get more oxygen into our lungs.

Even our brain needs oxygen or it just won't work. Our brain needs more oxygen than any other part of us. If the brain stops getting oxygen it has a brain attack. This is called a stroke. It's just like a heart attack, which happens when the heart stops getting blood with oxygen in it. To prevent a brain attack it is important to eat healthy foods and to exercise. Make sure your brain is working at its best by breathing in lots of oxygen.

1. Write the numbers 1 to 4 in the boxes to show the order of events.

- ☐ Oxygen goes into our lungs.
- ☐ The heart pumps the blood around the body.
- ☐ Humans breathe in oxygen.
- ☐ Oxygen goes into our blood.

Answers and explanations on pages 99–100

Mini Test 10 (continued)

2 What causes a stroke?
A the heart not getting blood
B being unfit
C eating unhealthy foods
D the brain not getting blood

3 Why do people puff and pant when exercising?
A to show off
B because they are tired
C because they are using all their muscles
D to get more oxygen

4 What part of the human body uses the most oxygen?
A muscles
B bones
C heart
D brain

5 You use oxygen faster when you are
A exercising.
B eating.
C sleeping.
D healthy.

6 This text is about
A what to do when you exercise.
B how our bodies use oxygen.
C how to exercise.
D how to be healthy.

Answers and explanations on pages 99–100

TIPS FOR WRITING

Check the Writing section (www.nap.edu.au/naplan/writing) **of the official NAPLAN website for up-to-date and important information on the Writing Test.** Sample Writing Tests and marking guidelines that outline the criteria markers use when assessing your writing are also provided. Please note that, to date in NAPLAN, the types of texts that students have been tested on have been narrative and persuasive writing.

The Australian Curriculum for English requires students to be taught three main types of texts that vary according to their purpose:

- imaginative writing (including narratives and poetry)
- informative writing (including procedures and reports)
- persuasive writing (expositions).

Informative writing has not yet been tested by NAPLAN. The best preparation for writing is for students to read a range of texts and to practise writing a wide variety of texts for different purposes. This book includes information on a variety of types of texts taught in the curriculum.

Persuasive texts

The purpose of a persuasive text is to persuade an audience about something. A persuasive text might argue a point of view or it might try to make you buy something or do something. A persuasive text has to be convincing. It needs to give clear reasons to make you agree with it.

Text structure

Introduction

The opening statement has to introduce the topic or issue. Make sure your audience knows your point of view or the point of view you are going to present about the topic.

Body

Present your arguments and reasons or evidence, in a logical sequence. Use one paragraph for each argument.

Conclusion

Make a summing up or concluding statement. Restate your point of view on the topic. You might add a recommendation or a call to action such as *Act NOW*!

Persuasive devices and vocabulary

Use words that are persuasive or forceful: *must*, *must not*, *should*, *shouldn't*.

Use adjectives: *beautiful*, *terrible*, *sweet*, *sour*.

Use adverbs: *extremely*, *sadly*, *very*, *really*.

Use commands: *Buy now! Act now! Stop! Don't do this!*

Narrative texts

A narrative is an imaginative text. It tells a story. Its purpose is mainly to entertain. Narratives can also teach lessons about life or help an audience think about an issue or point of view.

Narratives are written about characters. A narrative needs to make an audience feel something for its characters. We can like or dislike them, worry about them, understand how they are feeling or why they are acting the way they are. We can be happy for them, laugh at them or be angry with them.

Narratives can be written in the first person where the teller of the story is a character in the story.

Narratives can be written in the third person where someone outside the story, such as the author, is telling the story.

Text structure

Orientation

The orientation introduces the characters and the setting for the story. It sets the scene for the events that are about to take place.

Complication

The complication is the problem that occurs to complicate or upset the lives of the characters. Something goes wrong that needs to be sorted out or something unusual or out of the ordinary happens to the characters.

Plot

The body of the text is the plot. It consists of all the events that happen in the story, as characters sort out their problems.

Resolution

Stories need to have endings that make sense and satisfy readers. The characters' problem needs to be taken care of. Life needs to return to normal for the characters. This does not necessarily mean 'happily ever after'. Some stories have sad endings but readers understand that the characters will be all right. Characters often learn about themselves during the events in a story.

Language

Narratives use descriptive language, including adjectives and adverbs, to help readers imagine characters and settings. Readers build a mental picture of characters and settings. A mental picture is a picture in your mind.

Informative texts

Informative texts present information about a topic. Informative texts include reports, descriptions, news articles and features, bus timetables, shopping lists, recounts, explanations, menus, school rules and instruction manuals. Informative texts can be factual, as in a science report or recipe, or they can include opinions. For example, a personal recount presents information and can include the writer's opinions. Newspapers use descriptive language to make their reports sound more exciting or interesting.

Personal recount: text structure

Introduction

This section introduces or defines the topic. It tells the reader what the recount is going to be about.

Body

The main part of the text is called the body. In a recount the information is presented in time order. The recount starts with what happened first and then presents each event in a time sequence.

Conclusion

A concluding statement finishes off the recount. It can be a personal comment that tells how the writer feels about events or it can summarise the main information in the text.

Personal recount: language

Past-tense verbs are important in telling about things that have already happened.

Time words connect events and information in sequence: *this morning*, *then*, *after that*, *finally*, *later*.

The following tips are useful for Sample Writing Test 3 (page 83):

Description: text structure

An opening statement introduces the topic.

The body of the text provides details to help readers build a mental picture.

Description: language

Noun groups with adjectives describe the topic in detail.

Evaluative language provides opinions.

WRITING

Mini Test 1
Persuasive text

Before you start, make sure you read the Tips for Writing on pages 44–45.

Today you are going to write a persuasive text. The topic for your text is

People in cities should not be allowed to own dogs.

There are many people living in cities who own pet dogs. The dogs are good company for them. There are other people who think dogs don't belong in cities and should be banned altogether.

Before you start writing, think about:

- your opinion—whether you agree or disagree with the statement
- what reasons you can give to support your opinion.

Remember to:

- plan your writing
- use words that will convince a reader to agree with you
- use sentences
- check spelling and punctuation.

Start writing here.

Once the student has completed the Writing Test, turn to page 100 and use the Marking checklist to check the student's writing. Sample texts are included on pages 117–118. Discuss aspects of these model texts with the student, as appropriate.

WRITING

Mini Test 2
Narrative text

Before you start, make sure you read the Tips for Writing on pages 44–45.

Today you are going to write a narrative or story. The idea for your story is **LOST**.

People lose things every day. Things can disappear magically. People can get lost in real-life adventures. Story characters can get lost in the jungle, in another world or in outer space. Animals can get lost and have to find their way home.

Before you start writing, think about:

- who the story will be about
- where the story will take place
- what will happen to the characters
- how the story will end.

Remember to:

- plan your writing
- use sentences
- check spelling and punctuation.

Start writing here.

Once the student has completed the Writing Test, turn to page 101 and use the Marking checklist to check the student's writing. Sample texts are included on pages 119–120. Discuss aspects of these model texts with the student, as appropriate.

WRITING

Mini Test 3
Recount text

Before you start, make sure you read the Tips for Writing on pages 44–45.

Today you are going to write a recount. You will write about a trip that you have been on. Think about who you travelled with, how you travelled, where you went and what you did there. It could be a trip to the city, beach or countryside, a trip to visit a friend, a school excursion, or any other kind of trip.

Before you start writing, think about:

- an introduction to tell your readers what the recount is about
- the sequence of events—start with what happened first and then tell each event in a time sequence.

Remember to:

- plan your writing
- use sentences
- check spelling and punctuation.

Start writing here.

Once the student has completed the Writing Test, turn to pages 101–102 and use the Marking checklist to check the student's writing. Sample texts are included on pages 121–122. Discuss aspects of these model texts with the student, as appropriate.

SAMPLE NAPLAN ONLINE–STYLE LITERACY TESTS

DIFFERENT TEST LEVELS

- There are nine tests for students to complete in this section. These sample tests have been classified as either standard, intermediate or advanced according to the level of the majority of questions. This will broadly reflect the NAPLAN Online tailored testing experience where students are guided into answering questions that match their ability.
- The following tests are included in this section:
  - three Reading Tests at standard, intermediate and advanced levels
  - three Conventions of Language Tests at standard, intermediate and advanced levels
  - three Writing Tests.

CHECKS

- The NAPLAN Online Conventions of Language and Reading tests will be divided into different sections.
- Students will have one last opportunity to check their answers in each section when they have reached the end of that section.
- Once they have moved onto a new section, they will not be able to go back and check their work again.
- We have included reminders for students to check their work at specific points in the Sample Tests so they become familiar with this process before they take the NAPLAN Online tests.

Excel Test Zone

- After students have consolidated their topic knowledge by completing this book, we recommend they practise NAPLAN Online–style questions on our website at www.exceltestzone.com.au.
- Students will be able to gain valuable practice in online skills.
- Students will also become confident in using a computer or tablet to complete NAPLAN Online–style tests so they will be fully prepared for the actual NAPLAN Online tests.

Year 2 Conventions of Language

Sample Online-style Test 1

Standard level

1 Which word correctly completes this sentence?

I ______ quickly to the shop and bought milk.

A runned B running C ran D runner

2 Which pronoun correctly completes this sentence?

Molly and I like broccoli and ______ also like spinach.

A us B her C she D we

3 Which word correctly completes this sentence?

We kept our dog inside ______ she had a sore eye.

A so B because C until D but

4 Which word correctly completes this sentence?

Mum bought ______ some new running shoes.

A itself B himself C ourselves D herself

5 Which word in this sentence is a noun?

He sat on a comfortable chair.

A He B sat C comfortable D chair

6 Which word in this sentence is a verb?

The big wet dog slid across the floor.

A big B dog C slid D floor

7 Which word in this sentence is used as an adjective?

We ate the sweet strawberries with some cream.

A ate B sweet C strawberries D cream

8 In which sentence is there a mistake?

A I rided my bike to school today.
B Bike riding is good exercise.
C It's fun.
D I think I will ride to school tomorrow.

9 Which word correctly completes the sentence?

I ______ finished my homework.

A did
B have
C do
D has

Answers and explanations on pages 103–105

10 Which word in this sentence tells **how** to stir the mixture?

Dad said to stir the pancake mixture thoroughly.

A stir
B pancake
C mixture
D thoroughly

11 Which of these sentences is a command?

A Tie your shoelaces.
B Have your shoelaces come undone?
C I'll help you tie those shoelaces.
D It's dangerous to run with your shoelaces undone.

12 Which sentence is punctuated correctly?

A My hat is red
B my hat is red
C My hat is red.
D My hat is Red.

13 Which sentence is punctuated correctly?

A You're coming to my house after school?
B Will you come to my house after school?
C Maya is coming to my house?
D I'm allowed to go to your house?

14 Which sentence is punctuated correctly?

A Our teacher asked us to collect the bats, balls, stumps and helmets
B Our teacher asked us to collect the bats balls stumps and helmets.
C Our teacher asked us to collect the bats, balls, stumps, and helmets.
D Our teacher asked us to collect the bats, balls, stumps and helmets.

15 Which word is plural for baby?

A babies
B babys
C babes
D babeez

Answers and explanations on pages 103–105

16 Which of these words **cannot** be used to mean more than one?

A sheep

B people

C man

D fish

17 In which sentence is the word *of* used **incorrectly?**

A Ben ate a piece of pie.

C There was a dollop of cream on top.

B The pie was made of apples.

D He should of shared it with me.

18 Which sentence is correct?

A Me and Justin like our new teacher.

B Me and Justin likes our new teacher.

C Justin and I like our new teacher.

D Me and him like our new teacher.

19 Which sentence is punctuated correctly?

A Heidi and sally live in canberra.

B Heidi and Sally live in Canberra.

C Heidi and sally live in Canberra.

D heidi and sally live in Canberra.

20 Which word correctly completes this sentence?

The children ______ quiet.

A were

B was

C has

D is

21 The day before Saturday is

A Sunday B Monday C Thursday D Friday

and the day after Saturday is

E Sunday. F Monday. G Thursday. H Friday.

22 Draw lines to connect the adjectives to the correct nouns.

dry	skin
noisy	clothes
soft	tree
tall	magpies

Answers and explanations on pages 103–105

23 Write the words in the correct order to make a question.
eat / you / your banana / Did / for lunch / ?

24 Write each word in its correct column.
Ms Cheung, teacher, cat, Mr Whiskers, place, Tasmania

Common nouns	**Proper nouns**

25 Circle the correct article for each phrase.
A a / an goanna **B** a / an ape **C** a / an koala **D** a / an echidna

It would be a good idea to check your answers to questions 1 to 25 before moving on to the other questions.

To the student

Ask your teacher or parent to read the spelling words for you. The words are listed on page 129. Write the spelling words on the lines below.

26 ______ 27 ______

28 ______ 29 ______

30 ______ 31 ______

32 ______ 33 ______

34 ______ 35 ______

36 ______ 37 ______

38 ______ 39 ______

40 ______

Answers and explanations on pages 103–105

Read the sentences. The spelling mistake in each sentence is underlined. Write the correct spelling of the underlined word in the box.

41 Dad hurt his back doing the <u>gardning</u>.

42 Mum was <u>unnhappy</u> about the mess.

43 Spider <u>babys</u> are called spiderlings.

44 Rob is <u>takeing</u> us for a swim.

45 The cat jumped out and gave me a <u>frite</u>.

Each sentence has a word that is incorrect.
Write the correct spelling of the word in the box.

46 Lana throo the ball for the dog.

47 Brush yor teeth before bed.

48 Nia reads evry night.

49 The bath warter was too hot.

50 The book is four William.

Answers and explanations on pages 103–105

Intermediate level

1 Which word correctly completes this sentence?

Dad jumped too high on the trampoline and ______ off.

A fall B felled C fell D falling

2 Which pronoun correctly replaces the highlighted words in this sentence?

Mum took **Liam and me** to the movies.

A us B him C them D her

3 Which word in this sentence is a noun?

The cat was black and fluffy.

A The B cat C black D fluffy

4 Which word correctly completes this sentence?

Mum asked me to pass ______ the sauce.

A him B her C herself D she

5 Which word in this sentence is a verb?

Tommy ran quickly along the track.

A Tommy B ran C quickly D the

6 Which word in this sentence is used as an adjective?

The flowers growing all over the field were yellow.

A growing B all C field D yellow

The text below has some words missing. Choose the correct word to complete each sentence.

Text		A	B	C	D
Dad was talking ______ the telephone	7	in	at	on	to
______ his friend Mario.	8	to	at	of	by
Mario needed ______ help.	9	many	some	lots	for
He ______ moving furniture.	10	were	are	was	done

Answers and explanations on pages 105–106

11 In which sentence is there a mistake?

A The magpie swooped at my head.
B I is just walking past.
C It must have a nest nearby.
D I wonder how many eggs there are.

12 Which word correctly completes the sentence?

We waited until the light turned green ______ we crossed the road.

A so
B when
C until
D before

13 Which word in this sentence tells how Kirra ate?

Kirra ate quickly so she could go and play.

A Kirra
B ate
C quickly
D play

14 Which of these sentences is a command?

A Look!
B I need to be more careful.
C I love my new pencil case.
D Do you have new pencils?

15 Which sentence is punctuated correctly?

A the Plane took off for perth.
B The plane took off for Perth
C the plane took off for Perth.
D The plane took off for Perth.

16 Which sentence is punctuated correctly?

A What's the time?
B It's time for dinner?
C We should have dinner soon?
D We're hungry now?

17 Which sentence is punctuated correctly?

A Take Hugo for a walk, said Mum.
B "Take Hugo for a walk, said Mum."
C "Take Hugo for a walk, said Mum
D "Take Hugo for a walk," said Mum.

18 Which of the following is a sentence?

A Pencils and paper.
B We eat lunch at midday.
C Martin and me.
D Oranges, apples and pears.

19 Which sentence is punctuated correctly?

A Katy was born in June
B katy was born in June.
C Katy was born in June.
D Katy was born in june.

20 That book is better than this one.

In this sentence the word *one* is used instead of

A book.
B person.
C author.
D library.

Answers and explanations on pages 105–106

21 The day before Sunday is

A Monday B Thursday C Friday D Saturday

and the day after Sunday is

E Saturday. F Monday. G Thursday. H Friday.

22 Draw lines to connect the adjectives to the correct nouns.

happy	fence
icy	baby
strong	moon
full	drink

23 Write the words in the correct order to make a command.

. / the grass / up / on / Line /

____

____

24 Write each word in its correct column.

dog, Emma, city, German Shepherd, Melbourne, girl

Common nouns	**Proper nouns**
______________	______________
______________	______________
______________	______________
______________	______________

25 Write the correct article for each phrase.

A _______ dingo B _______ bee C _______ lemon D _______ elephant

It would be a good idea to check your answers to questions 1 to 25 before moving on to the other questions.

Answers and explanations on pages 105–106

Year 2 Conventions of Language Sample Online-style Test 2

To the student

Ask your teacher or parent to read the spelling words for you. The words are listed on pages 129–130. Write the spelling words on the lines below.

26 ______ 27 ______

28 ______ 29 ______

30 ______ 31 ______

32 ______ 33 ______

34 ______ 35 ______

36 ______ 37 ______

38 ______ 39 ______

40 ______

Read the sentences. The spelling mistake in each sentence is underlined. Write the correct spelling of the underlined word in the box.

41 Zac had to <u>ansa</u> the question.

42 Henry made a <u>misstake</u> in spelling.

43 Mum is <u>begining</u> to play the piano.

44 I am going to the movies in the <u>holadays</u>.

45 I'm going to the dentist <u>nekst</u> week.

Each sentence has a word that is incorrect. Write the correct spelling of the word in the box.

46 Our dance teacha is from Somalia.

47 Shut the door, pleez.

48 Lana is my frend.

49 I sit beside Rina in clarss.

50 We lookt for the ball in the grass.

Answers and explanations on pages 105–106

Year 2 Conventions of Language

Sample Online-style Test 3

Advanced level

1 Which pronoun correctly completes this sentence?

I love my mum because ______ is wonderful.

A her B she C they D you

2 Which word correctly completes this sentence?

We'll leave early ______ we have plenty of time.

A until B before C firstly D so

3 Which word correctly completes this sentence?

We sat ______ the dinner table for lunch.

A in B on C onto D at

4 Which word in this sentence is a verb?

The owl swooped onto the field mouse.

A The B owl C swooped D field

5 Which word in this sentence is used as an adjective?

It was a really hot day last Saturday.

A really B hot C last D Saturday

The text below has some words missing. Choose the correct word or words to complete each line.

6	In ______ emergency dial 000.	A a	B an	C its	D his
7	When ______ call is answered	A my	B her	C his	D your
8	______ ready to tell the operator	A have	B is	C be	D are
9	what kind ______ emergency	A in	B of	C on	D by
10	______ the address.	A so	B while	C because	D and

11 In which sentence is there a mistake?

A The children walked to the shop.
B They had to buy bread for sandwiches.
C Mum said they could also bought ice-creams.
D They were very excited.

12 Which of the following is a sentence?

A Go to school. B His and hers.
C Last Monday Dad and I. D Muddy footprints on the carpet.

Answers and explanations on pages 107–108

13 Which word in this sentence is an adverb that tells **how**?

The silkworm chomped slowly on the juicy leaf.

A silkworm B chomped C slowly D juicy

14 Which sentence is punctuated correctly?

A We went to the library
B We went to the library.
C we went to the library.
D We went to the Library

15 Which sentence is punctuated correctly?

A Sit at your desks?
B Have you finished your work?
C Talk quietly?
D I wonder where the cat is hiding?

16 Which sentence is punctuated correctly?

A Rose took off her socks, shoes and raincoat.
B Rose took off her socks shoes and raincoat.
C Rose took off her, socks, shoes, and raincoat.
D Rose took off her socks, shoes and raincoat

17 Which conjunction joins the clauses correctly?

I did my homework quickly ______ I wanted to go out to play.

A and B but C so D because

18 Which word in this sentence is a common noun?

He bit into the juicy watermelon.

A bit B into C juicy D watermelon

19 Which sentence is punctuated correctly?

A The name of my school is glendale primary school.
B the name of my school is Glendale Primary School
C The name of my school is Glendale Primary School.
D The Name of my school is Glendale primary school

20 Which sentence is punctuated correctly?

A "I saw a flying saucer," said Louie.
B "I saw a flying saucer, said Louie."
C I saw a flying saucer, "said Louie".
D "I saw a flying saucer, said Louie.

21 Choose the correct answers to correctly complete the sentence.

We should take our umbrellas

A so B but C because D and

it might rain

E so F but G because H and

we'll be outside for most of the day.

Answers and explanations on pages 107–108

22 Match the nouns and pronouns by drawing lines.

Ms Barton	it
Mr Walsh	she
the children	he
the ball	they

23 Write the words in the correct order to make a question.

/ for breakfast / you / ? / did / What / have /

____

____

____

24 Write a word that tells **how** alongside each verb.

loudly, carefully, greedily, swiftly

Verb	**Adverb that tells how**
ran	______________
laughed	______________
ate	______________
listened	______________

25 Circle the noun group It refers to in the text.

The hungry tiger walked quietly through the long grass. It was looking for prey.

It would be a good idea to check your answers to questions 1 to 25 before moving on to the other questions.

Answers and explanations on pages 107–108

Year 2 Conventions of Language Sample Online-style Test 3

To the student

Ask your teacher or parent to read the spelling words for you. The words are listed on page 130. Write the spelling words on the lines below.

26 ____________ 27 ____________

28 ____________ 29 ____________

30 ____________ 31 ____________

32 ____________ 33 ____________

34 ____________ 35 ____________

36 ____________ 37 ____________

38 ____________ 39 ____________

40 ____________

Read the sentences. The spelling mistake in each sentence is underlined. Write the correct spelling of the underlined word in the box.

41 Billy said the fish tastid funny.

42 My granperants live in Manly.

43 It's impossable to beat Harriet in a swimming race.

44 Mum mowed the lorn.

45 The bread was stail.

Each sentence has a word that is incorrect.
Write the correct spelling of the word in the box.

46 The lion sat on a rock with a liness.

47 A feemale horse is a mare.

48 A male chicken is a roosta.

49 A female focks is a vixen.

50 A baby horse is a fole.

Year 2 **Reading**

Sample Online-style Test 1

Standard level

Read the email and answer questions 1 to 6. Circle the correct answers.

Delete | Reply | Reply All | Forward | Flag | Unread | Read | New Message | Get Mail | Note | To Do

From: Jordan H
To: peterlouisa@online.com.au

Hi Mum and Dad

I am having a great time with my grandparents. Nonno and I take Jack for a walk to the beach every day. Jack loves it. He chases seagulls and fetches sticks that Nonno throws into the water.

Nonno likes to cook. His favourite dish is Spaghetti alla Pescatore. That's spaghetti with seafood. We both love it but I don't like the clams. I just like it with prawns and calamari.

Nonna is busy every day at the shop with Aunty Maria. Nonna says it's good that I can keep Nonno busy during the school holidays. Then Nonno doesn't get into mischief. Grandparents are funny.

I miss you.
Love Jordie

1 Who are Nonno and Nonna?
- **A** Jordie's parents
- **B** Jordie's grandparents
- **C** Jordie's aunt and uncle
- **D** friends of the family

2 Jack is
- **A** Nonno's dog.
- **B** Nonna's friend.
- **C** Jordie's uncle.
- **D** Jordie's grandpa.

3 Which ingredients do **not** belong in *Spaghetti alla Pescatore*? Choose two.
- **A** spaghetti
- **B** seafood
- **C** seagulls
- **D** sticks

4 Where does Nonna work?
- **A** in a school
- **B** in a shop
- **C** in a restaurant
- **D** She doesn't work.

5 Which is **not** true about Nonno?
- **A** He works in a shop with Aunty Maria.
- **B** He likes to walk along the beach.
- **C** He likes to cook.
- **D** He likes to get into mischief.

6 Jordie would describe Nonno as
- **A** lazy.
- **B** boring.
- **C** fun.
- **D** cranky.

Answers and explanations on pages 108–109

Year 2 Reading Sample Online-style Test 1

Read the report *Celebrating with food* and answer questions 7 to 12. Circle the correct answers.

Celebrating with food

People around the world use food in celebrations. There are many types of food used in this way.

ANZAC biscuits are eaten in New Zealand and Australia, especially on ANZAC Day (25 April). ANZAC biscuits were made during World War I and shipped overseas for the soldiers to eat. ANZAC biscuits are made with oats.

Oranges and tangerines are important fruit at Chinese New Year. In Chinese New Year festivities they represent a long, healthy life and happiness.

A noodle dish called 'kook soo' is served in the traditional Korean wedding banquet called 'kook soo sang', meaning 'noodle banquet'. Long noodles represent a long marriage and a long life.

A piñata is a container, made to hold small items such as sweets. It can be made of pottery, papier-mâché or fabric. Piñatas are used in Mexico in celebrations such as birthdays. The piñata is hung from a branch of a tree or the ceiling and people hit it to break it open so all the goodies fall out.

La Tomatina is a famous tomato-squishing–and-throwing festival. La Tomatina is held in Spain each August. The rules of the festival say that tomatoes must be squished before thrown, so that no one gets hurt.

7 Which of the following is used to make ANZAC biscuits?

A oranges
B tomatoes
C oats
D cheese

8 Which fruit is important for celebrating Chinese New Year?

A apples
B tangerines
C bananas
D kiwi fruit

9 What is 'kook soo sang'?

A a long life
B a noodle dish
C a noodle banquet
D a Korean wedding

10 Piñatas are usually filled with

A sweets.
B pottery.
C fabric.
D fruit.

11 Choose two answers. Noodles are used in a wedding feast as a lucky symbol for

A tasty food.
B a long life.
C a great celebration.
D a long marriage.
E good luck.

12 Which is **not** true?

A A tomato festival rule says to squish tomatoes before throwing them.
B It's important to hurt people with tomatoes.
C At La Tomatina you only throw squished tomatoes.
D The tomato festival is held in August each year.

It would be a good idea to check your answers to questions 1 to 12 before moving on to the other questions.

Answers and explanations on page 109

Read the chart and answer questions 13 to 18. Circle the correct answers.

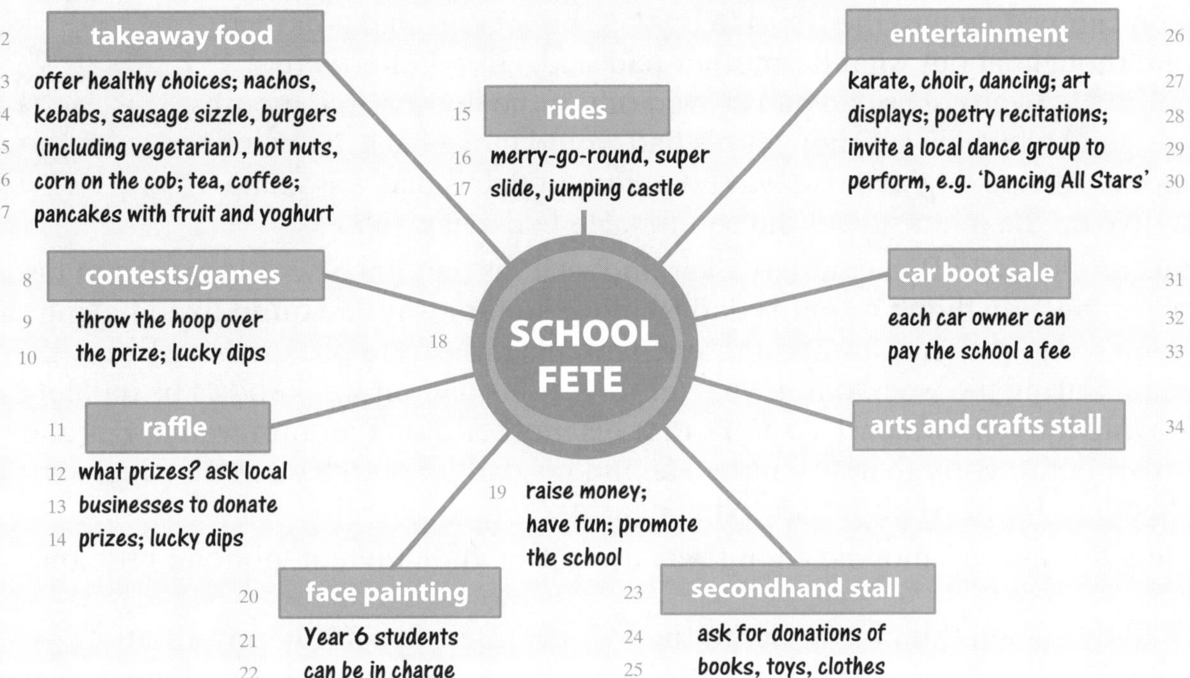

13 What is brainstorming?
- **A** writing a report on a topic
- **B** creating a list of ideas on a topic
- **C** using your brain to think about the school fete
- **D** the teacher writing ideas on a whiteboard

14 Who will be in charge of face painting?
- **A** Year 6 students
- **B** parents
- **C** teachers
- **D** volunteers

15 How will the pancakes be served?
- **A** any way you like
- **B** with fruit and yoghurt
- **C** with jam and cream
- **D** with honey and banana

16 What is the name of the dance group that could perform at the fete?
- **A** karaoke
- **B** Dancers
- **C** Dancing All Stars
- **D** Sunshine Dancers

17 How will the car boot sale raise money for the school?
- **A** People will sell goods out of their cars.
- **B** People will make donations.
- **C** The cars will park in the school grounds.
- **D** The school will charge a fee for each car.

18 What will local businesses be asked to do?
- **A** build a new fence
- **B** donate raffle prizes
- **C** face painting
- **D** run a car park

Answers and explanations on page 109

Year 2 Reading Sample Online-style Test 1

Read the narrative *Long-distance dad* and answer questions 19 to 24. Circle the correct answers.

Long-distance dad

Ben climbed up into the tree. He hooked his legs around a branch and thought about what his mother had said. His parents were getting a divorce. His dad had moved out of the house three months ago but he had always thought his dad would move back. Now his mother was saying that dad was gone for good. His dad was going to live on the other side of the country. He had a new job.

His mother said Ben could fly over and visit his dad once he was settled in his new place but Ben didn't want his dad to move so far away. He quite liked having two homes, one with his mother and one with his father. He preferred to live with his mum during the week but it was fun to visit his dad on weekends. His dad let him stay up late and watch TV shows that his mother didn't let him watch. His dad was also a better cook than his mum. He and his dad liked to try out new recipes together. He liked his father living nearby.

Now his dad was moving a long way away. Ben didn't like it, not one little bit.

19 What was Ben thinking about in the text?
A falling out of the tree
B his homework
C his parents' divorce
D watching TV shows

20 How long ago did Ben's father move out of the family home?
A ages ago
B not long ago
C yesterday
D three months ago

21 What activity did Ben like to do with his father?
A play computer games
B cook
C climb
D fly in aeroplanes

22 Ben was not happy about
A his dad moving a long way away.
B having two homes.
C his mother not letting him watch
D being stuck in the tree.
some TV shows.

23 Ben's dad was moving away because
A he wanted to live on the other side of the country.
B he was getting a divorce.
C he couldn't live with Ben's mother any more.
D he had a new job.

24 Another title for the text could be
A How to climb trees safely.
B Ben and his mum have a talk.
C Cooking with Dad.
D Separation.

It would be a good idea to check your answers to questions 13 to 24 before moving on to the other questions.

Year 2 Reading Sample Online-style Test 1

Read the report *The Tasmanian devil* and answer questions 25 to 31. Circle the correct answers or draw lines.

The Tasmanian devil

Tasmanian devils live in Tasmania. They are marsupials. Marsupials are animals that have pouches for their babies.

Tasmanian devils have black fur. Some can have white patches of fur on their chest or neck.

Tasmanian devils are carnivores. Carnivores eat meat. Devils eat small mammals, birds, lizards and frogs. They will even eat dead things that they find. They have wide, strong jaws for eating bones and fur. Devils fight with each other over food. Some have battle scars from fights.

Tasmanian devils are nocturnal. This means they are active at night. They hide during the day. Devils make a number of sounds, including a scary screeching sound which early settlers in Tasmania found frightening.

Tasmanian devils are suffering from a disease that causes cancers to grow around the face and mouth. This disease has killed a large number of devils over the last twenty years. Devils are also killed by cars, dogs and foxes.

25 Tasmanian devils live in

A trees.
B Australia.
C Tasmania.
D the forest.

26 What is a marsupial?

A an animal that carries its young in a pouch
B an animal from Tasmania
C a Tasmanian devil
D an animal that has black fur

27 Choose two answers. Tasmanian devils eat

A dead things. **B** fruit.
C wood. **D** meat.
E grass.

28 Why do Tasmanian devils have strong jaws?

A for chewing bones and fur
B for digging dens
C to kill frogs
D to fight with each other over food

29 How are Tasmanian devils killed?

A by cars, dogs and foxes
B by eating dead animals
C by cars, dogs, foxes and disease
D by other Tasmanian devils

30 What is the purpose of the text?

A to entertain
B to inform
C to persuade people to help Tasmanian devils
D to tell people about Tasmania

31 Draw lines to link the adjectives to the correct nouns from the text.

Adjective	Noun
strong	animal
pouched	screeching
scary	fur
white	jaws
black	patches

Answers and explanations on page 110

Year 2 Reading Sample Online-style Test 1

Read the poster *Down came the spider* and answer questions 32 to 39. Circle the correct answers.

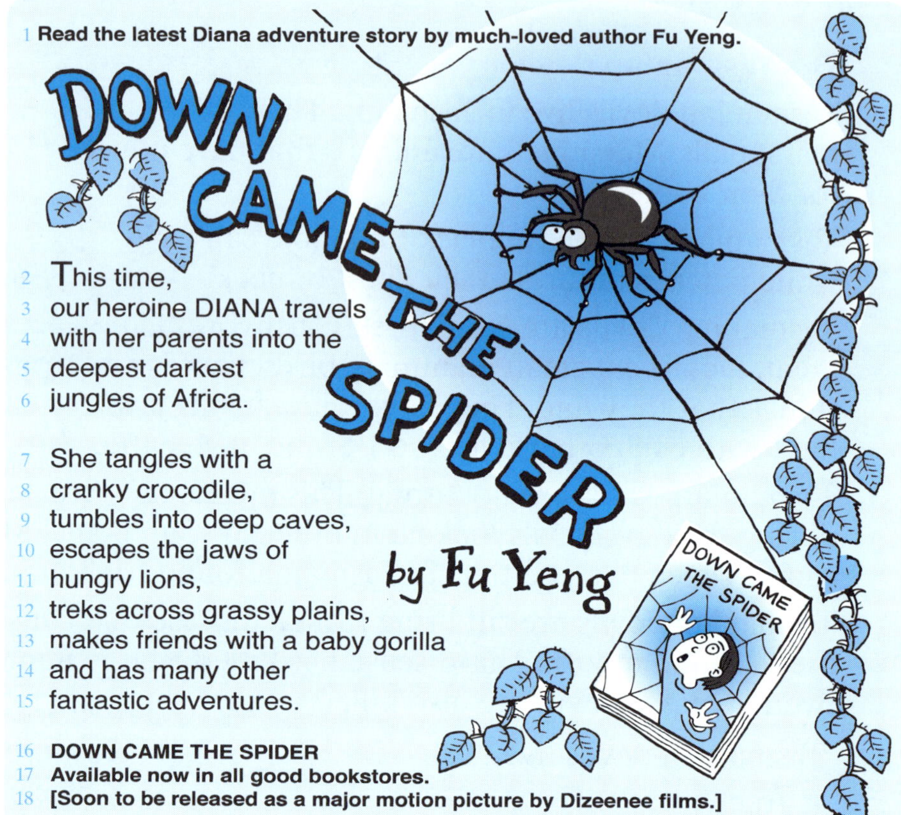

32. Who is the author of the book *Down Came the Spider*?
   A Diana
   B Fu Yeng
   C Diana's parents
   D Dizeenee Films

33. The main purpose of this poster is to
   A summarise the story *Down Came the Spider.*
   B tell people about the importance of books.
   C describe Africa.
   D convince people to read *Down Came the Spider.*

34. *… many other fantastic adventures*
   The text says this to show that *Down Came the Spider* is
   A full of action. **B** sad. **C** funny. **D** realistic.

35. What does the text tell you about Diana?
   A She is adventurous. **B** She is shy.
   C She is funny. **D** She is always hungry.

36. The setting for *Down Came the Spider* is
   A a bookstore. **B** a spiderweb. **C** Africa. **D** Australia.

37. Do you think you would like to read *Down Came the Spider?* Write your answer on spare paper, giving a reason.

38. What does *latest* mean in *Read the latest Diana adventure story …* ?
   A Diana has lots of adventures.
   B This is the most recent book in a series of books about Diana.
   C Fu Yeng writes lots of books.
   D Readers cannot believe how many adventures Diana has.

39. Find four action verbs in the text that begin with the letter ***t***.

Answers and explanations on pages 110–111

Year 2 Reading

Sample Online-style Test 2

Intermediate level

Read *How to prevent tooth decay* and answer questions 1 to 6. Circle the correct answers.

How to prevent tooth decay

Teeth have a hard outer layer of tooth enamel. This enamel helps to protect teeth.

When you don't clean your teeth properly your teeth get covered in plaque.

Plaque is made up of sugars, bits of food, and bacteria that live in your mouth.

Bacteria eat the sugars and make acid. The acid destroys tooth enamel. Then you get holes in your teeth.

Brushing your teeth twice a day helps to remove the plaque. Flossing your teeth also helps to remove the plaque. If you can't brush your teeth after eating you should rinse your mouth with water. Sugary foods and soft drinks are particularly bad for your teeth.

Using fluoride toothpaste helps strengthen tooth enamel and protect teeth.

1 Tooth enamel

- **A** is plaque.
- **B** fights sugar.
- **C** fights bacteria.
- **D** protects teeth.

2 You can strengthen tooth enamel by

- **A** using fluoride toothpaste.
- **B** eating hard foods.
- **C** brushing and flossing.
- **D** rinsing with water.

3 Bacteria in your mouth make

- **A** teeth.
- **B** sugar.
- **C** acid.
- **D** plaque.

4 Acid destroys

- **A** bacteria.
- **B** tooth enamel.
- **C** plaque.
- **D** holes.

5 Which is **not** true?

- **A** Prevent tooth decay by eating less sugary food.
- **B** Prevent tooth decay by brushing and flossing.
- **C** Prevent tooth decay by using fluoride toothpaste.
- **D** Prevent tooth decay by covering your teeth in plaque.

6 Brushing teeth

- **A** flosses them.
- **B** puts holes in them.
- **C** removes plaque.
- **D** destroys tooth enamel.

Answers and explanations on page 111

Year 2 Reading Sample Online-style Test 2

Read the narrative *A frog's lament* and answer questions 7 to 12. Circle the correct answers or write an answer.

A frog's lament

One day a tiny little frog, only two and a half centimetres long, leapt onto a leaf and called, "Squelch!" It did not hear any of its kind calling back.

"Where is everyone?" it called again.

It leapt from leaf to rock and rock to leaf searching for other Corroboree frogs.

Finally, it heard a small call. It stopped and there it found a tiny tadpole, lying in a small pool of water.

"Where is everyone?" the frog asked.

The tadpole sobbed. "I don't know where the frogs are but this pool of water is getting too small for me. I need to grow my arms and legs very soon and turn into a frog."

A small voice called out to them from under a leaf. "The fungus killed the frogs," it said. Another Corroboree frog crept out. "The fungus got on their skin. They're dead. And climate change is making the weather too warm. The water pools are drying out too quickly. The tadpoles don't have time to turn into frogs. They're dying too."

"What can be done?" lamented the first little frog.

7 How big was the frog?

A not very big
B two and a half centimetres
C two centimetres
D too small

8 What kind of frog was it?

A tadpole
B fungus
C Corroboree frog
D tiny little

9 The tadpole was

A warm.
B hungry.
C happy.
D upset.

10 Why does the tadpole need to turn into a frog very soon?

A so it won't die when the water dries out
B so it can jump
C so it can search for food
D so that it can help find other frogs

11 What did the fungus do?

A It stopped the tadpoles from turning into frogs.
B It killed the frogs.
C It killed the tadpoles.
D It changed the climate.

12 How would you answer the frog's final question?

____

____

It would be a good idea to check your answers to questions 1 to 12 before moving on to the other questions.

Answers and explanations on page 111

Year 2 Reading Sample Online-style Test 2

Read the information on the graph and answer questions 13 to 18. Circle the correct answers.

Our favourite-fruit graph

Students in our class voted for their favourite fruit. The top eight fruits are shown on the graph. Students made their decisions based on taste but also on how easy it was to eat the fruit. Some students didn't like fruit with seeds. Others said that bananas went soggy too easily when packed in lunchboxes but were wonderful when perfectly ripe. All but two students like banana splits for dessert. One student has a friend who is allergic to bananas. Some students said that they like tinned fruit best but most said that they love fresh fruit as well as dried and tinned fruit.

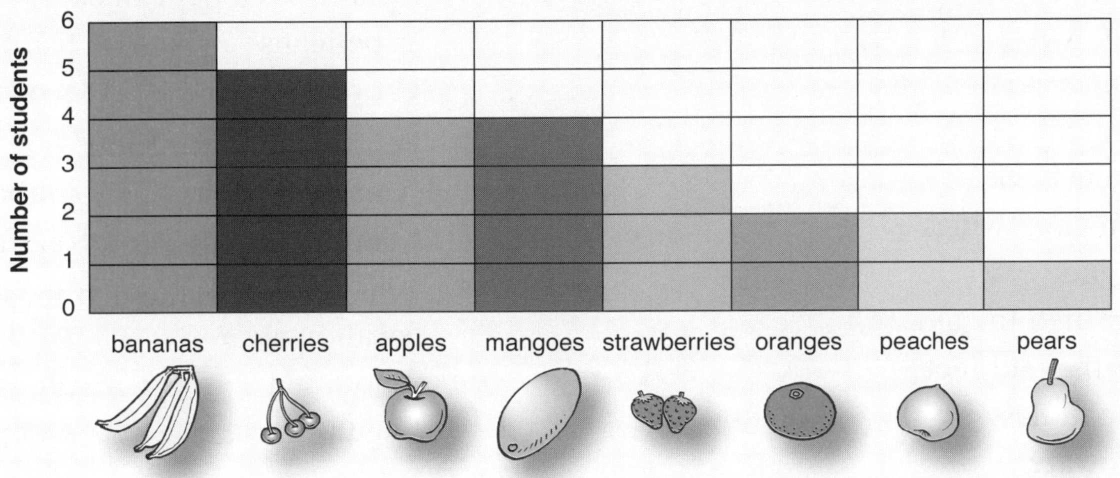

13 How many students prefer oranges?

A 1 B 2 C 3 D 4

14 Which is the most popular fruit in the class?

A cherries B bananas
C mangoes D strawberries

15 Which is the least popular fruit on the graph?

A peaches B apples
C mangoes D pears

16 Most students said they like fruit that is

A fresh.
B ripe.
C fresh, dried or tinned.
D dried and tinned.

17 Why are bananas not popular with some children at school?

A because they cause allergic reactions
B because they get soggy in lunchboxes
C because they make school bags smelly
D because they don't taste as good as other fruit

18 The graph shows

A which fruit is most popular with children in the class.
B which fruit is the least popular with the children.
C which fruit can be tinned and dried.
D which fruit is best for lunchboxes.

Answers and explanations on page 111

Year 2 Reading Sample Online-style Test 2

Read the poem *Pelican* by Tanya Dalgleish and answer questions 19 to 25. Circle the correct answers or draw lines.

Pelican

The
pelican—
magnificent bird.
Big belly.
Big feet.
Big eyes.
Big bill.
Long neck.
On giant wings
it glides
through the air.
With giant feet
it paddles
on water.
Looking for food
it plunges its bill
under the surface.
Scooping the fish
into its pouch
then
gulping them
down
head first.
Belly now full,
it rests
on a lamp post,
looking out
on the world
from its great lofty height—
amazing.

19 The words *magnificent* and *amazing* tell readers that the poet

A is frightened of pelicans.
B doesn't like pelicans.
C is impressed by pelicans.
D thinks pelicans are too big.

20 What does a pelican eat?

A pelicans B fish
C bread D seeds

21 Pelicans look for food

A at the beach. B in the water.
C in the air. D on the sand.

22 Which word in the text means 'swallowing'?

A looking B plunges
C gulping D scooping

23 Which word tells how the pelican moves through the air?

A floats B glides
C paddles D rests

24 What is the main idea in the poem?

A Pelicans are a nuisance.
B Pelicans look strange.
C Pelicans eat too many fish.
D Pelicans are terrific birds.

25 Draw lines to link the adjectives to the correct nouns.

Adjective	**Noun**
lofty	bird
full	neck
giant	height
magnificent	belly
long	feet

It would be a good idea to check your answers to questions 13 to 25 before moving on to the other questions.

Answers and explanations on page 112

Year 2 Reading Sample Online-style Test 2

Read *A trip to the museum* and answer questions 26 to 32. Circle the correct answers.

A trip to the museum

Yesterday, all the children in my class went on an excursion to the museum.

When we arrived at the museum we met the museum curator. He told us all about the paintings we were going to see. He told us that the paintings were by artists from the Warakurna community. He said that Warakurna is in the middle of Australia, about 330 kilometres west of Uluru. He showed us on a map.

After the talk we looked at the Warakurna paintings. The paintings were of everyday events as well as events in Warakurna history. One painting showed a group of women from Warakurna performing at the opening ceremony of the Sydney Olympic Games in 2000. We learned a lot about the lives of the Warakurna people from looking at these paintings. It was really interesting.

Our school canteen had packed us a picnic lunch of sandwiches, fruit and water. We ate lunch outside the museum entrance. Then we caught our bus back to school. We arrived back at school just in time for assembly.

26 How did the children travel to the museum?

A by car
B by bus
C by train
D on foot

27 A museum curator

A drives a school bus to museums.
B is an artist.
C knows all about the items in a museum.
D makes school lunches.

28 The purpose of the text is to

A describe Aboriginal artworks.
B tell about an event that has happened.
C describe what the children had for lunch.
D tell a story.

29 The writer of the text is

A a child in the class.
B the school principal.
C a parent volunteer.
D the museum curator.

30 Warakurna is located

A near the museum.
B at Uluru.
C in Sydney.
D in the middle of Australia.

31 Where did the children eat lunch?

A outside the museum
B in the museum
C on the lawn in a park
D during school assembly

32 The writer would judge the excursion to have been

A boring.
B useless.
C worthwhile.
D an exciting adventure.

Answers and explanations on page 112

Year 2 Reading Sample Online-style Test 2

Read *Our adventure playground* and answer questions 33 to 39. Circle the correct answers.

Our adventure playground

There is a playground in town that I love. It is the best playground I have ever seen. It was built last year. It has flying foxes, super slides, a rock-climbing wall, a spider-web climbing frame, a huge sandpit, swings, slippery dips and spinners.

There is also a bicycle track. The older children like the bike track.

There is a water play area, mainly for toddlers. Frog fountains spurt out water. Little children have a great time splashing under the frogs.

There are plenty of barbecues. Families can have sausage sizzles and spend the whole day at the park. There are lots of shade trees and sheltered picnic tables. You can also buy hot food, drinks and ice creams, at the nearby kiosk.

The playground won an award last year for best playground design. I recommend our adventure playground to all families with children of any age. Entry is free.

33 How does the writer feel about the playground?

A disappointed B excited
C upset D angry

34 The frog fountains are mainly enjoyed by

A frogs. B older children.
C toddlers. D parents.

35 The purpose of the text is to tell readers

A how to get to the playground.
B how good the playground is.
C how to build a playground.
D about food they can buy at the playground.

36 The bike track is popular with

A parents.
B toddlers.
C whole families.
D older children.

37 How much does it cost to use the playground?

A nothing B a small fee
C a parking fee D a lot

38 What type of people would enjoy the park? Choose the best answer.

A families with toddlers
B families with older children
C teenagers
D families with children of all ages

39 Compare two texts. *Our adventure playground* is

A informative B imaginative
C persuasive

and *A trip to the museum* (page 73) is

D informative. E imaginative.
F persuasive.

Answers and explanations on pages 112–113

Year 2 Reading

Sample Online-style Test 3

Advanced level

Read *Recycling glass* and answer questions 1 to 6. Circle the correct answers or write an answer.

Recycling glass

Recycling means 'reusing things'. Glass can be reused over and over and over again.

1. People throw glass bottles and jars into recycling bins.
2. The glass is taken to a recycling plant.
3. The glass is sorted according to colour, either clear, brown or green (the colouring agent in glass cannot be removed so brown glass will always be recycled as brown glass, and green as green glass).
4. The glass is cleaned to remove dirt, bits of plastic, metal or other non-glass products.
5. The glass is crushed—crushed glass is called 'cullet'.
6. The cullet is melted and mixed with sand, soda ash and limestone, then moulded into new bottles and jars.

It is quick and easy to recycle glass and cheaper than making new glass. Recycling glass saves lots of carbon dioxide from going into the air. Carbon dioxide is a greenhouse gas. Greenhouse gases are unhealthy for planet Earth.

1 Recycling means

A reducing greenhouse gases.
B cycling instead of driving.
C making new bottles and jars out of used bottles and jars.
D reusing things.

2 Write the numbers 1 to 4 in the boxes to show the order of events in the text. The first one has been done for you.

☐	Cullet is melted.
☐	Glass is cleaned.
☐	Glass is crushed to make cullet.
1	Glass is sorted by colour.

3 What is *cullet*?

A crushed glass B brown glass
C recycled glass D clean glass

4 Green glass will always be recycled as

A bottles and jars. B brown glass.
C clear glass. D green glass.

5 Which is **not** true?

A Recycling saves lots of carbon dioxide from going in the air.
B Recycling saves money.
C Recycling is difficult.
D Glass can be recycled again and again.

6 What is the writer's opinion about glass recycling?

A It is a process that turns waste products into new usable products.
B It is good for planet Earth.
C It is difficult to sort out the different colours of glass.
D People don't recycle enough glass.

Answers and explanations on page 113

Year 2 Reading Sample Online-style Test 3

Read *Clever birds* and answer questions 7 to 12. Circle the correct answers.

Clever birds

Crows, rooks and ravens make up the 'corvid' family of birds. Corvids are really clever. They have big brains for their size. They use their clever brains to solve problems. Corvids use tools such as sticks to get food from cracks in rocks. They have been seen placing nuts on roads so that cars squash the shells open. Some crows in Japan have shown they understand how traffic lights work. They place nuts on the road to be run over by cars. Then they wait for the traffic lights to turn red so the cars stop. Then the birds collect their crushed nuts while it's safe.

One crow was seen dropping rocks into a jar of water. It kept adding rocks until the water level rose. A floating worm was lifted within reach of the crow's beak. That's clever!

People have seen corvids playing with each other. They have also been seen playing tricks on other animals. Some people have seen ravens steal dog toys and hide them from the dogs then watch as the dogs search for their toys.

Some farmers say that corvids kill their lambs but mostly crows and ravens just clean up dead animals. This includes lambs that have died during birth and animals killed by cars.

7 Corvids are a bird family that includes
A black eagles.
B owls.
C ravens.
D pelicans.

8 What does the text tell you about corvids?
A They are black birds.
B They are clever birds.
C They are friendly birds.
D They live in Australia.

9 A corvid might use a stick to
A poke a pet dog.
B have a sword fight with another corvid.
C scratch its back.
D get food from a crack in a rock.

10 Which is **not** true?
A Some corvids play tricks.
B All farmers hate corvids.
C Corvids use tools.
D Corvids are problem-solvers.

11 How did the Japanese crows use traffic lights?
A to know when to cross the road
B to know when it was safe to collect their crushed nuts
C to crack open nuts
D to teach other crows about road safety

12 What happened when the crow dropped stones in a jar of water?
A It got splashed.
B It could see a worm floating there.
C It ate a worm.
D The water level rose.

It would be a good idea to check your answers to questions 1 to 12 before moving on to the other questions.

Answers and explanations on pages 113–114

Read the letter *Dear Zoo* and answer questions 13 to 18. Circle the correct answers.

Dear Zoo

Amira Salim
42 Flinders Drive
Padstow NSW 2211

Management
Taronga Zoo
Bradleys Head Road
Mosman NSW 2088

To whom it may concern

I visited Taronga Zoo yesterday and I loved the wonderful chimpanzee home. Chimpanzees are my favourite animals.

My mum says that zoo animals don't get very well looked after in some parts of the world. I want to thank you for looking after all your animals so well.

I think chimps would be really bored in a cage or small enclosure where there is nothing for them to do. The chimps at Taronga have a wonderful place to play.

I would love to work with animals one day, especially chimps. I hope I can be a zoo keeper and work at Taronga Zoo. Mum says that she will buy me a Zoo Friends Membership for my birthday. She loves Taronga Zoo too.

Thank you again.

Yours sincerely
Amira Salim

13 Amira wrote the letter to
- A tell a story about chimpanzees.
- B give her opinion about the zoo.
- C ask for a job at the zoo.
- D persuade people to visit the zoo.

14 Which word tells you that Amira liked the chimpanzee home?
- A wonderful
- B chimpanzee
- C home
- D favourite

15 Choose two answers. When Amira grows up she wants to
- A go to zoos all over the world.
- B be a zoo keeper.
- C be a chimpanzee.
- D have a birthday party.
- E work at Taronga Zoo.
- F be a mother chimpanzee.

16 What does Amira's mother think about Taronga Zoo?
- A She told Amira to write a letter to the zoo.
- B She doesn't like zoos.
- C She loves Taronga Zoo.
- D She wants Amira to be a zoo keeper.

17 What is Amira getting for her birthday?
- A a Zoo Friends Membership
- B a bike
- C a toy chimpanzee
- D paper and pencils

18 The letter makes the reader
- A feel sorry for chimpanzees.
- B feel angry.
- C worry about animals in zoos.
- D feel good about Taronga Zoo.

Answers and explanations on page 114

Read *Jackie and the magic seeds* and answer questions 19 to 24. Circle the correct answers.

Jackie and the magic seeds

Early one morning Jackie's dad asked her to go to the shop. He told her to buy two tomatoes for dinner. He gave her $1. At the shop, tomatoes cost more than $1 each so Jackie could not afford to buy even one. She left the shop.

On the way home Jackie met a man who was selling tomato seeds. Jackie read the sign, 'Tomato seeds: 10 seeds for one dollar. Fast growing.' Jackie asked the man if the tomatoes would grow in time for dinner. The man said yes, they definitely would. So, Jackie bought the seeds.

When she showed the seeds to her father he was very angry. He said that Jackie had been tricked and that the seeds were useless. He said that the tomatoes would never grow in time for dinner and now they would go to bed hungry. He threw the seeds out the window.

Jackie went outside to find her seeds. To her astonishment she discovered that the seeds had already started to grow. Ten tomato plants had sprouted up from the ground where the seeds had landed. They kept growing in front of her eyes. Their thick stalks grew so quickly that before long their tips had disappeared into the clouds. Jackie wondered what was at the top of the stalks. She looked for a foothold.

19 What did Jackie buy at the shop?
- A two tomatoes
- B one tomato
- C tomato seeds
- D nothing

20 Why was Jackie's father angry?
- A Jackie did not buy tomatoes.
- B He thought Jackie had been tricked.
- C He was hungry.
- D Tomatoes cost too much.

21 What did Jackie's father do with the seeds?
- A He threw them out the window.
- B He planned to have tomatoes for dinner.
- C He planted them in the garden.
- D He told Jackie they were useless.

22 What does astonishment mean?
- A anger
- B surprise
- C amusement
- D sorrow

23 What is the purpose of the text?
- A to explain how seeds grow
- B to entertain
- C to teach children not to be tricked
- D to complain about the cost of tomatoes

24 What do you think will happen next in the story?
- A Jackie and her father will go to bed hungry.
- B Jackie's father will chop down the plant.
- C Jackie will climb the tomato stalks.
- D Jackie and her father will have tomatoes for dinner after all.

It would be a good idea to check your answers to questions 13 to 24 before moving on to the other questions.

Answers and explanations on page 114

Read *Note to Fred* and answer questions 25 to 31. Circle the correct answers or draw lines.

Note to Fred

Hi Fred

I'm supposed to go to Grandma's house today. My mother asked me to take Grandma a basket of cookies but I am in bed with the flu. Please, will you go and check on my grandma and take her the cookies? I have drawn you a map to help you find her house. It's on the other side of the forest. It's an easy walk but watch out for wolves.

Thank you very much.

Your Friend,

Red

25 Who is Fred?

A a next-door-neighbour
B Red's father
C Red's grandpa
D Red's friend

26 What does Red want Fred to do for her?

A check on Grandma and take her cookies
B take Grandma a basket of cookies
C find Grandma's house on the other side of the forest
D look after her because she is sick

27 Red tells Fred to watch out for

A the forest.
B wolves.
C cookies.
D Grandma.

28 How will Fred recognise Grandma's house?

A It has a red door.
B It is on the other side of the forest.
C It says Grandma lives here.
D It's an easy walk.

29 Where does the wolf like to hide?

A at Grandma's house
B up a tree in the forest
C behind the biggest tree
D anywhere along the main path

30 How does Red describe the walk to Grandma's?

A dangerous
B scary
C easy
D dark

31 Draw lines to link the adjectives to the correct nouns.

Adjective	**Noun**
sick	tree
sneaky	walk
easy	wolf
biggest	friend
good	girl

Answers and explanations on page 115

Year 2 Reading Sample Online-style Test 3

Read *Olympics* and answer questions 32 to 39. Circle the correct answers.

Olympics

The Olympic Games and the Paralympic Games are held every four years. The best athletes in the world come together and compete for their countries.

I like watching the gymnastics and hockey in the Summer Olympics best. I like the gymnastics because the athletes are so fit and flexible. I like the hockey because it is fast and exciting. The rules are a lot like soccer, which I play, so it's easy to follow the game.

My brother is in Year 5. He likes to watch long-jump events because he competes in long jump in our school athletics carnivals.

My sister likes the swimming relays. She says that the relays are the most exciting of all the swimming events. She also likes the running relays, especially the 100-metre race.

Mum really likes it when a developing country in Africa wins a medal. Most of those countries don't have a lot of money to spend on athletes. They don't win very many medals. It's fantastic when they win. Mum likes to cheer for the underdog.

32 How often are the Olympic Games held?
- A every three years
- B every four years
- C when the best athletes in the world come together
- D when countries decide to have them

33 Why does the writer like to watch hockey?
- A It's fast and exciting.
- B The players are fit and flexible.
- C The writer's brother and sister don't watch the hockey.
- D The best athletes compete.

34 What Olympic events does the writer's sister like to watch?
- A long jump
- B running and swimming relays
- C gymnastics and hockey
- D athletics

35 The writer's brother competes in
- A long jump.
- B athletics.
- C swimming.
- D hockey.

36 What does it mean to *cheer for the underdog*?
- A cheering for dogs
- B cheering for countries in Africa
- C cheering for somebody who is not expected to win
- D cheering for somebody who likes dogs

37 The purpose of this text is to
- A convince readers that the Olympics are good to watch.
- B describe all the different sports at the Olympics.
- C tell a story about playing sport.
- D share opinions about the Olympics.

38 Which sport does the writer participate in?
- A hockey
- B gymnastics
- C soccer
- D swimming

39 Which statement best summarises the text?
- A Families enjoy watching the Olympics.
- B Mum loves to see African countries win medals.
- C People enjoy watching, and competing in, different sports.
- D The writer loves exciting and energetic sports best.

Answers and explanations on page 115

Sample Test 1

Before you start, make sure you read the Tips for Writing on pages 44–45.

Today you are going to write a persuasive text.
The topic for your text is

All schools should have a swimming pool.

Before you start writing, think about:
- your opinion—whether you agree or disagree with the statement
- your reasons.

Remember to:
- plan your writing
- write your opinions and reasons
- write in sentences
- use words that will convince a reader to agree with you
- check spelling and punctuation.

Start writing here.

☞ Once the student has completed the Writing Test, turn to page 100 and use the Marking checklist to check the student's writing. Sample pieces of writing are included on pages 123–124. Discuss aspects of these model texts with the student, as appropriate.

Sample Test 2

Before you start, make sure you read the Tips for Writing on pages 44–45.

Today you are going to write a narrative or story. The idea for your story is

Into another world.

In fantasy stories, characters journey into other worlds. The other world can be through a magical doorway, inside a mirror, at the top of a tree or down a rabbit hole. Story characters can find strange creatures in the other world and have adventures before returning home. What magical world would you like to visit? How would you enter this magical world? What would you find there? What would you do before returning home?

Before you start writing, think about:

- the setting for your story
- the characters
- what happens in the story
- how the story will end.

Remember to:

- plan your writing
- use sentences
- check spelling and punctuation.

Start writing here.

Once the student has completed the Writing Test, turn to page 101 and use the Marking checklist to check the student's writing. Sample pieces of writing are included on pages 125–126. Discuss aspects of these model texts with the student, as appropriate.

Year 2 Writing

Sample Test 3

Before you start, make sure you read the Tips for Writing on pages 44–45.

Today you are going to write a **description**. Write about something you know really well. You could describe your home, your bedroom, a person, a pet, a place that you visit, or anything else you choose.

Before you start writing, think about:

- an introduction to tell your readers what the description is about
- how you will sequence the information
- adding personal comments.

Remember to:

- plan your writing
- use sentences
- check spelling and punctuation.

Start writing here.

Once the student has completed the Writing Test, turn to page 116 and use the Marking checklist to check the student's writing. Sample pieces of writing are included on pages 127–128. Discuss aspects of these model texts with the student, as appropriate.

Mini Test Answers

Standard level questions

SPELLING Mini Test 1

Page 1

1 two **2** classroom **3** You **4** put **5** write
6 went **7** like **8** said **9** name **10** park
11 eggs **12** nest **13** bird **14** insect **15** hive
16 gather **17** They **18** make

1 *Two* is the word for the number or numeral 2. *Two, to* and *too* are homophones. Homophones sound the same but are spelt differently and mean different things. Learn the difference between *two* (2), *to* (e.g. Go to the shop) and *too* (e.g. I'll come too).

2 *Classroom* is a compound word. Compound words are made by joining two individual words, e.g. *playground, shoelace, football*. Be careful not to put ***r*** in *class*.

3 *You* is a common word that you need to remember how to spell.

4 The ***u*** in *put* makes the sound found in *push, butcher* and *full*.

5 *Write* starts with a silent ***w***. The ***i*** makes a long ***i*** sound. The ***i*** is a long vowel—it says its own name—because the word ends in the silent ***e***. When words end in a single consonant and a final ***e*** the middle vowel makes a long vowel sound. *Write* is a homophone for *right*.

6 *Went* is a common word. Each letter makes its usual sound. Be careful not to confuse it with the 'wh' spelling in *when*.

7 *Like* has an ***i–e*** combination that makes the ***i*** say its own name in the word.

8 *Said* has 'ai' which makes a short ***e*** sound. Learn to spell this word because it is very useful when writing conversation in your own texts.

9 *Name* has a long ***a*** sound because the ***a*** is followed by a consonant and a silent ***e***.

10 *Park* ends in ***k*** rather than 'ck'. It rhymes with *dark, mark* and *stark*.

11 *Eggs* is a plural word. Plural means 'more than one of something'. *Eggs* ends in ***s*** which sounds like *z*. Many plurals end in the *z* sound: *logs, beds* and *legs*.

12 *Nest* is a simple four-letter/four-sound word that is spelt the way it can be sounded out.

13 *Bird* has 'ir' which is also used in *birthday, thirst* and *dirt*. Other words spell the 'ir' sound differently: *heard, verb, worse* and *journey*.

14 *Insect* ends in 'ct' which is also used in *object, direct* and *reflect*.

15 *Hive* has an ***i–e*** pattern. The final ***e*** makes the ***i*** say its own name in the word.

16 *Gather* has a 'th' that sounds the same in *brother, bother* and *other*.

17 The 'ey' in *they* is also found in *obey* but very few other words. There are many ways to spell the same sound: *day, break* and *eight*.

18 *Make* has a long ***a*** sound because the ***a*** is followed by a consonant and an ***e*** (***a–e*** pattern). *Make* rhymes with *cake, stake, rake, mistake* and *shake*.

SPELLING Mini Test 2

Page 2

1 girl **2** boys **3** asleep **4** This **5** Today
6 again **7** little **8** look **9** how **10** when
11 four **12** feet **13** finger **14** sunny **15** bus
16 water **17** over **18** crabs

1 *Girl* starts with a hard ***g*** sound. The 'ir' is used in *birth, bird* and *dirt*.

2 *Boys* contains the letters 'oy', also found in *toy* and *enjoy*. The sound made by 'oy' in *boy* is spelt 'oi' in *oil*.

3 The 'ee' in *asleep* makes the long ***e*** sound, also spelt 'ee' in *cheep, keep, feet, meet, see* and *tree*.

4 *This* is a common word. The 'th' sounds the same as in *they, there* and *then*.

5 *Today* ends in 'ay' which rhymes with *stay, pay, hay, may, ray* and *delay*.

6 *Again* is sometimes pronounced 'agen' but it is spelt with 'ai'.

7 *Little* ends in 'le' as in *settle, peddle, saddle, pickle, gentle* and *rattle*. Be careful not to confuse it with words that end in 'al': *medal, petal* and *metal*.

8 *Look* has the same 'oo' sound as in *cook, book, chook* and *took*.

9 *How* is spelt with 'ow' as in *cow* and *brown*. Be careful because 'ou' can spell the same sound in *out, mouth* and *drought*.

10 *When* uses 'wh' as in *where, what, which* and *why*.

11 *Four* is a number word that has the homophones *fore* and *for*. Homophones sound the same but have different meanings and are spelt differently.

12 *Feet* is the plural for the singular word *foot*. It uses 'ee' as in *sheet, sleet, fleet* and *sleep*.

13 *Finger* ends in 'er' as in *linger, shoulder* and *robber*.

14 *Sunny* has the consonant ***n*** doubled (nn) before ***y*** is added to make an adjective from *sun*. Double the final ***n*** in *fun* and *run* to add ***y*** for *funny* and *runny*.

15 *Bus* is a simple three-letter word that is spelt the way it sounds.

16 *Water* has the letter ***a*** which sounds like 'aw' or 'or'. The same sound and spelling can be found in *wall, call* and *also*.

17 *Over* is spelt using 'er'.

18 *Crabs* starts with a hard ***c*** rather than a ***k***.

Intermediate level questions

SPELLING Mini Test 3

Page 3

1 beach **2** police **3** pulled **4** Our **5** outside **6** slow **7** running **8** teeth **9** wish **10** school **11** door **12** chair **13** table **14** rice **15** butter **16** stir **17** coconut **18** salt

1 *Beach* uses 'ea' to make a long ***e*** sound. Other 'ea' words are *peach, teach* and *bean*.

2 Pronounce the word *police* carefully to hear the sound made by ***o***. Remember that *police* ends in 'ice'.

3 *Pulled* has a ***u*** as in *push, butcher* and *full*. Other words have the same vowel sound but are spelt differently, e.g. *book, could*.

4 *Our* is pronounced 'owr'. Other words spelt with *our* are *hour* and *flour*.

5 *Outside* is spelt with 'ou' as in *shout, mouth, loud* and *proud*. *Outside* is a compound word. It is made up of two smaller words: *out* + *side*.

6 *Slow* rhymes with *blow, show, grow* and *mow*. The same long ***o*** vowel sound in *slow* can be spelt 'ou' as in *though* and *dough*; 'oa' as in *boat* and *goat;* or 'oe' as in *toe*.

7 The rule for words with a short vowel that end in a single consonant (e.g. run, hop, shop) is to double the final consonant before adding the suffix 'ing', e.g. *running, hopping* and *shopping*.

8 *Teeth* is the plural for the singular word *tooth*. Pronounce it properly to hear the 'th' ending. *Teeth* uses 'ee' as in *sleep*.

9 *Wish* uses ***w*** rather than 'wh'.

10 The 'ch' in *school* makes a ***k*** sound.

11 *Door* rhymes with the word *or* but is spelt with a double ***o*** as in *poor* and *floor*. Be careful not to confuse it with words that have 'aw', e.g. *raw, paw* and *law*.

12 The 'air' sound in *chair* has the same spelling as in *fair, pair* and *air*. Other ways to spell the same sound can be found in *their, there, pear* and *square*.

13 *Table* ends in 'le' as in *whistle, settle, kettle, apple, giggle, puddle* and *tickle*.

14 *Rice* ends in 'ice', like *nice* and *lice*. It has a soft ***c*** sound. The final ***e*** makes the ***i*** vowel a long vowel, saying its own name in the word. Other soft ***c*** words that end in ***e*** are *lettuce, reduce, dance* and *prance*.

15 *Butter* ends in 'er' as in *gather, lather* and *feather*.

16 The 'ir' in *stir* can be found in *birthday, thirsty, dirty* and *bird*. The sound can be spelt with 'er' as in *verb* or 'ur' as in *curb*.

17 Each ***c*** in *coconut* makes a hard ***k*** sound as in *cucumber, car* and *correct*.

18 The sound made by ***a*** in *salt* sounds like the ***a*** in *what* and *was*.

SPELLING Mini Test 4

Page 4

1 birthday **2** many **3** chased **4** climb **5** says **6** teacher **7** homework **8** some **9** stank **10** writing **11** clock **12** skipping **13** boat **14** toes **15** eyes **16** knees **17** brain **18** nose

1 *Birthday* has the same 'ir' combination as *dirt, shirt, thirst* and *first*. Make sure you pronounce the 'th' correctly and not as ***f***.

2 *Many* is spelt with an ***a*** that sounds like an ***e***. The same spelling can be found in *any* and *says*. The ***y*** on the end of the word *many* sounds like *funny, runny, sunny, honey* and *money.*

3 *Chased* is a past-tense regular verb that ends in the suffix 'ed'**.** When adding 'ed' to words that already end in ***e*** (as in *chase*), simply add ***d***, e.g. *share* → *shared, hope* → *hoped*.

4 *Climb* has a silent ***b*** on the end. *Lamb* and *thumb* also end in a silent ***b***.

5 *Says* is spelt with an ***a*** that makes a short ***e*** sound but *say* has a long ***a*** sound and rhymes with *day*. Note the different pronunciation of the ***a*** in *say* and *says* in these sentences: *I heard him say that he liked bananas. He says he likes bananas.*

6 *Teacher* is spelt with 'ea' which has the long ***e*** sound as in *peach, reach, cheat, repeat* and *eat*. Words for occupations often end in 'er', e.g. *gardener, cleaner, lawyer, baker* and *butcher* but can also end in 'or', e.g. *doctor* or 'ist', e.g. *dentist*.

7 *Homework* is a compound word: *home* + *work*. The 'or' makes the same sound in *worm*.

8 *Some* and *sum* are homophones. They sound the same but are spelt differently and mean different things. *Sum* is a word used in maths to mean 'adding up' or 'a total'. *Some* means 'an indefinite number of things'.

9 *Stank* is a past-tense irregular verb. *It stinks* → *It stank*. Irregular verbs form the past tense by changing their spelling in some way other than adding 'ed'. The 'nk' can be found in *dunk, pink, chunk* and *plank*.

10 *Writing* is formed from *write* + 'ing'. When adding 'ing' to words that end in ***e*** drop the final ***e***, e.g. *hope* → *hoping, drive* → *driving*.

11 *Clock* is spelt with a hard ***c*** at the beginning and a final 'ck'. It rhymes with *dock, shock, flock* and *stock*.

12 *Skipping* is a verb that doubles the final consonant before adding the suffix 'ing'. Other verbs that add 'ing' in this way include *running, hopping, putting* and *sitting*.

13 The 'oa' in *boat* sounds like a long ***o***, e.g. *float* and *oat*. Be careful not to confuse it with 'ow' words such as *row, grow* and *show*.

14 The 'oe' in *toes* makes a long ***o*** sound, also spelt in the following ways: *goat, show, note, dough*.

15 *Eyes* is a common word that you need to learn how to spell by sight rather than by sounding it out.

16 *Knees* begins with a silent ***k*** as in *knife, knock* and *know*.

17 *Brain* has the 'ai' vowel pattern which says a long ***a*** sound, also in *drain, pain, rain, gain* and *stain*. Be careful not to confuse its spelling with the long ***a*** sound made by ***a–e*** words, e.g. *name, game, shame, pane* and *plane*.

18 *Nose* has the long ***o*** sound made by the ***o–e*** combination. This combination can be found in *hose, rose, chose, note, dome, stone, bone, zone, home, lone* and *vote*.

SPELLING Mini Test 5

Page 5

1 because **2** remembered **3** apple **4** word **5** itchy **6** blue **7** chew **8** Tuesday **9** Wednesday **10** Monday **11** small **12** night **13** quick **14** asked **15** anybody **16** Somebody **17** Everybody **18** doctor

1 *Because* is a common word. Learn to spell it automatically.

2 *Remember/ed* has the suffix 'ed' which is added to *remember* to make it past tense.

3 *Apple* ends in 'le' as in *table, whistle, settle, kettle, apple, giggle, puddle, tickle* and *popsicle*.

4 The 'or' in *word* says 'er'. Other words with the same sound and spelling are *worm* and *worse*. Watch out for 'er' words as in *verb*, 'ear' words as in *earth,* and 'ir' words like *dirt;* they make the same vowel sound but use different spellings.

5 Pronounce *itchy* carefully and you will notice the ***t*** sound before the 'ch'. *Itchy* ends in a ***y*** that sounds the same as the ***y*** in *dirty, happy, baby, silly* and *lazy*.

6 The 'ue' in *blue* sounds like 'oo' in *boot*, 'ou' in *you*, 'ew' in *chew*, 'oe' in *shoe* and 'ui' in *fruit*. The 'ue' spelling can also be found in *glue*.

7 *Chew* is spelt like *grew, blew, flew, brew, dew* and *spew*.

8 *Tuesday* has a 'ue' that makes a long ***u*** sound. Learn the 'ue' spelling of *Tuesday* when you learn to spell *blue, glue* and *true*. Remember that days of the week are proper nouns and need capital letters. *Day* rhymes with *pay, say* and *lay*.

9 *Wednesday* has a silent ***d***.

10 In *Monday* the ***o*** sounds like a short ***u***. This ***o*** can be found in *money, honey, mother, love* and *come*.

11 *Small* rhymes with *all, ball, tall, fall* and *stall*. Remember its spelling by using 'sm' in front of *all*.

12 In *night* the 'igh' makes one sound like a long ***i***. Rhyming words with the same spelling include *fright, sight* and *light*.

13 *Quick* starts with 'qu'. Most words using 'qu' say a 'kw' sound.

14 *Asked* has the 'ed' suffix for a past-tense verb. There is no ***r*** in *ask*. The same 'ah' sound and spelling is found in *bath, path* and *past*.

15 *Anybody* is a compound word. It is made up of two smaller words: *any* + *body*. Don't be tricked: *any* starts with ***a***, as in *many* and *says*.

16 *Somebody* is a compound word. The ***o*** in *some* sounds like a ***u***.

17 *Everybody* is a common word. Look for the word *ever* in *every*.

18 *Doctor* is an occupation word that ends in 'or' like *actor, author* and *sail*or. The ***c*** in *doctor* is hard and makes the ***k*** sound.

SPELLING Mini Test 6

Page 6

1 ticket **2** toast **3** lamb **4** your **5** What **6** watched **7** screamed **8** suddenly **9** leaves **10** power **11** loud **12** friend **13** baby **14** house **15** are **16** Saturday **17** large **18** tomatoes

1 *Ticket* ends in the same final sound as *pocket, locket, packet, racket* and *billet*.

2 The 'oa' in *toast* makes a long ***o*** sound. The same spelling is used for the long ***o*** sound in *boat, goat, float, throat* and *moan*.

3 *Lamb* ends in a silent ***b***. Other silent ***b*** words are *thumb* and *comb*.

4 *Your* sounds like 'yor'. Remember that *your* has *you* in it.

5 *What* starts with 'wh' that sounds the same in *whistle, which, where, when, why* and *whether*. Sometimes the same sound can be made with ***w*** on its own, e.g. *water, wave* and *win*.

6 The ***a*** in *watched* says a short ***o*** sound as in *what* and *was*. The suffix 'ed' is used to make the verb past tense.

7 'Scr' is a three-letter combination that can be found in *scratch, script, scrap* and *screen*.

8 There is no ***r*** in *suddenly*. An 'ly' is added to the end of words so that they tell how: *sudden* + 'ly'. You will find the spelling easier if you think about the word without the 'ly' suffix.

9 The 'ea' says a long ***e*** sound in *leaves*. *Bean* and *teacher* have the same 'ea' spelling. Other letter combinations make a long ***e*** sound, e.g. 'ee' in *feet*, 'ie' in *piece*, 'ei' in *ceiling* and ***i*** in *machine*.

10 The sound made by 'ow' in *power* is the same as in *cow, brow, brown, down, frown, crown* and *drown*. The 'er' ending can be found in *flower, driver, never, shiver* and *river*.

11 *Loud* has an 'ou' also found in *proud* and *cloud*.

12 *Friend* is a common word. You need to learn to spell the 'ie'. Most words have ***i*** before ***e*** except after ***c***, as in *receive*.

13 *Baby* ends in ***y*** that says the 'ee' sound, also found in *funny, happy, silly* and *holly*.

14 *House* uses the same 'ou' digraph found in *loud, out, mouth, flour* and *sour*.

15 *Are* is a very common verb. You need to remember how to spell it automatically.

16 *Saturday* is a proper noun name for a day of the week. It uses 'ur' as in *turf, burn, churn* and *return*.

17 *Large* has a soft ***g*** because the ***g*** is followed by ***e***.

18 *Tomatoes* is the plural word for *tomato*. Remember that *tomatoes* ends in 'toes'. Words ending in a consonant and then ***o*** often form plurals by adding 'es', e.g. *potatoes* and *mangoes*.

Advanced level questions

SPELLING Mini Test 7

Page 7

1 ice **2** happiest **3** noise **4** parents **5** people **6** strawberries **7** wishes **8** trouble **9** using **10** rectangle **11** shoulders **12** could **13** machine **14** recipe **15** potatoes **16** onions **17** fast **18** burn

1 *Ice* has a soft ***c*** because ***c*** is followed by ***e***. *Ice* is found in *rice, dice, splice, thrice, twice* and *suffice*.

2 When adding suffixes to words that end in ***y*** you often need to change the ***y*** to an ***i*** before adding the suffix, e.g. *silly* → *silliest, crazy* → *craziest, funny* → *funniest*.

3 *Noise* has an 'oi' combination that is found in *oil, toil, foil* and *boil*. The same sound is spelt 'oy' in *enjoy* and *boy*.

4 *Parents* is a plural word. Plural words mean 'more than one'.

5 *People* is plural for *person*. *People* and *person* start with 'pe'. *People* ends in 'le' as in *apple, topple, grapple, staple* and *sample*.

6 *Strawberries* is plural for *strawberry*. Nouns ending in ***y*** usually change ***y*** to ***i*** to add 'es' when forming the plural, e.g. *cherry* → *cherries, lolly* → *lollies, baby* → *babies*. The 'aw' spelling in *straw* can be found in words that rhyme, e.g. *draw, raw* and *paw*.

7 *Wishes* is plural for *wish*. Many nouns add 'es' to form plurals, e.g. *dish* → *dishes, peach* → *peaches, dress* → *dresses, lunch* → *lunches*.

8 *Trouble* is spelt with 'ou' which sounds like a short ***u*** as in *touch, tough* and *rough*. It ends in 'le' like *rumble, tumble, thimble* and *tremble*.

9 Words ending in ***e*** often drop the ***e*** before adding the suffix 'ing', e.g. *use* → *using, write* → *writing, bite* → *biting*.

10 *Rectangle* ends with 'gle' as in *jungle, bungle* and *tangle*. It is spelt with a ***c*** not a ***k***.

11 *Shoulders* is spelt with 'ou' as in *boulder* and *mould*.

12 *Could* is a common word. It rhymes with *would* and *should*. The ***l*** is silent.

13 *Machine* has 'ch' which makes a 'sh' sound. This sound is also made in words with the suffix 'tion', e.g. *motion* and *nation*.

14 *Recipe* has a soft ***c*** because ***c*** is followed by ***i***.

15 Most common nouns ending in ***o*** add 'es' to form the plural, e.g. *potatoes, tomatoes* and *volcanoes*.

16 *Onions* sounds as if it starts with a short ***u*** sound. The letter ***o*** also says the short ***u*** sound in *mother, honey, money, worry, come* and *done*.

17 There is no *far* or ***r*** in *fast*. Try saying the word with an American accent to help you remember to spell it ***f–a–s–t***.

18 The 'ur' in *burn* can be found in *turn, churn, return, nurse* and *fur*. Be careful not to confuse the 'ur' spelling pattern with 'er' in *her* and *fern*, 'ir' in *birthday*, 'or' in *word* and *work*.

SPELLING Mini Test 8

Page 8

1 brother **2** usually **3** whole **4** neighbour **5** Neither **6** laughed **7** yesterday **8** heard **9** women **10** Where **11** squirted **12** hurt **13** person **14** Thursday **15** favourite **16** monkey **17** young **18** cared

1 Remember that 'bro' is slang for *brother* and you will remember to use ***o*** in *br<u>o</u>ther*.

2 Pronounce *usually* carefully. Spell *usual* and then add the suffix 'ly'.

3 *Hole* and *whole* are homophones. They sound the same but are spelt differently and have different meanings. *Annie ate the whole mango* means she ate all of it. A *hole* is a space or an opening.

4 In *neighbour* the 'eigh' makes one long ***a*** sound. It is also used in *eight, weight* and *weigh*.

5 Spell *Neither* with 'ei' rather than 'ee'. Note that in most words ***i*** comes before ***e*** but *neither* and *either* are exceptions to the rule. *Neither* is always used with *nor* in sentences. *Neither Mum nor Dad can come to the meeting*. *Either* is always used with *or*. *Either Mum or Dad will come to the meeting*.

6 The 'au' in *laugh* says 'ar'. The 'gh' says ***f***. *Laughed* ends in the suffix 'ed'.

7 Pronounce *yesterday* correctly and notice there is no ***a*** sound in the middle. There are three syllables in *yes–ter–day*. There is no double ***s*** in *yesterday*.

8 *Herd* and *heard* are homophones. They sound the same but have different meanings and spellings. The word *hear* is in *heard* which is to do with hearing noise. A *herd* is a group of animals such as cows.

9 *Women* is an irregular plural. Irregular plurals are formed in a different way from adding ***s*** or 'es', e.g. *goose* → *geese, mouse* → *mice, person* → *people, man* → *men, foot* → *feet*. Some nouns are always plural and have no singular, e.g. *scissors, pyjamas* and *clothes*.

10 *Where* and *wear* are homophones. *Where* is a common word to learn to spell automatically. The 'ere' in *where* says 'air'. Other ways to spell the 'air' sound include 'are' as in *rare, stare, bare* and *fare*, 'ear' as in *bear* and *pear*, 'air' as in *stair* and *chair*.

11 *Squirted* is a past-tense verb. It uses 'qu' to say 'kw'. Watch out for the 'ir' combination. Don't confuse it with 'ur' as in *burn* and *hurt*, or 'er' as in *fern* and *learn*.

12 *Hurt* has the same 'ur' spelling as *churn, burn, return, spur* and *turnip*.

13 *Person* is a singular noun. Its plural is *people*. Remember that *person* and *people* start with 'pe'.

14 *Thursday* is a proper noun for a day of the week. It has the 'ur' combination found in many words. See **12** above.

15 *Favourite* is tricky because it contains 'our' in the middle and has a silent ***e*** on the end.

16 *Monkey* ends in 'key' as in *turkey* and *donkey*. Note that the 'mo' in *monkey* sounds the same as *money*.

17 *Young* has an 'ou' that says the short ***u*** sound. It is used in *touch, couple, trouble* and *courage*.

18 *Cared* is a past-tense verb: *care* + 'ed'. Words ending in ***e*** drop the ***e*** to add 'ed', e.g. *shared, glared, spared, raked* and *baked*.

SPELLING Mini Test 9

Page 9

1 hugged **2** catch **3** shoes **4** fourth **5** tried **6** eighth **7** cried **8** forgotten **9** ninth **10** welcome **11** impossible **12** irresponsible **13** hopeless **14** fruit **15** soup **16** coming **17** minutes **18** hurry

1 When adding a suffix to a single-syllable word with one vowel then one consonant at the end (hug), you usually double the final consonant, e.g. *hug, hugged, hugging; fit, fitted, fitting; sit, sitting*. Note that words ending in ***w***, ***x*** or ***y*** never have the last letter doubled, e.g. *mix → mixed, sew → sewing, say → saying.*

2 *Catch* has three sounds: ***c–a–***'tch'. Remember the ***t*** in words such as *witch, ditch, watch, stitch, pitch* and *glitch*.

3 In the plural noun *shoes* the 'oe' says 'oo'. Another 'oe' word that sounds the same is *canoe*. The same sound is spelt differently in these words, e.g. *boot, soup, chew, through, blue* and *juice.*

4 *Fourth* is made from the number *four*. Remembering this will help you spell it correctly. The homophone *forth* means *forward.*

5 *Tried* is a past-tense verb from *try*. When adding suffixes such as 'ed' to words that end in ***y*** change the ***y*** to ***i*** before adding 'ed'.

6 *Eighth* is formed by adding the suffix 'th' to the number *eight*. The final ***t*** is dropped first.

7 Most words ending in a consonant and then a ***y*** (cry) change ***y*** to ***i*** to add most suffixes except 'ing', e.g. *cry, cries, cried, crying; dry, dries, dried, drying; tidy, tidier, tidiest, tidying.*

8 *Forgotten* is formed from the verb *forget*. The syllable 'got' has a vowel then a consonant and so the final consonant is doubled before adding the suffix 'en'.

9 *Ninth* is made from the number *nine*. Drop the ***e*** when adding the 'th' suffix.

10 *Welcome* loses the second ***l*** from *well* when combining with *come*. Most one-syllable words ending in a double ***l*** lose an ***l*** to add a word beginning with a consonant, e.g. *altogether, already.*

11 *Impossible* begins with 'im' which is a negative prefix. It is added to the beginning of words to make opposites: *possible → impossible.*

12 *Irresponsible* begins with 'ir' which is a negative prefix. It is added to the beginning of words to make opposites: *responsible → irresponsible.*

13 *Hopeless* ends with the suffix 'less' which means 'without'. *Hopeless* means 'without hope'.

14 *Fruit* uses 'ui' to spell the 'oo' sound. This sound appears with different spellings in *boot, flute, move, shoe, soup* and *glue.*

15 *Soup* uses 'ou' to spell the 'oo' sound. This sound appears with different spellings in *boot, flute, move, shoe, glue* and *fruit.*

16 *Coming* ends with the suffix 'ing'. Most words with the ***o–e*** pattern drop the ***e*** before adding 'ing', e.g. *hoping, doping* and *coping.*

17 *Minutes* is a plural noun. Note that the ***u*** makes a short ***i*** sound.

18 *Hurry* ends in a ***y*** which makes the same sound in *furry, silly, baby* and *handy.*

SPELLING Mini Test 10

Page 10

1 females **2** guitar **3** we're **4** prawns **5** beautiful **6** woolly **7** special **8** answers **9** nicely **10** wolves **11** buses **12** pieces **13** scary **14** author **15** frightened **16** exciting **17** worry **18** know

1 *Females* is a plural feminine noun. Its opposite is *males.* Other gender words include *boy–girl, man–woman, goose–gander, cow–bull* and *stallion–mare.*

2 *Guitar* is tricky. Note the ***u*** before the ***i.***

3 *We're* is a contraction for *we are*. *Mum said we are going* ... The apostrophe (') marks the place of the letter ***a*** which was left out when the words were joined and shortened.

4 *Prawns* is spelt with 'aw' as in *raw, saw* and *draw.*

5 *Beautiful* uses the suffix 'full' to mean 'full of beauty'. When adding 'full' as a suffix you only usually need one ***l***, e.g. *hopeful, dreadful*. Remember the sequence of the three vowels 'eau'.

6 *Woolly* is an adjective made from the noun *wool* and the suffix 'ly'.

7 In *special* the ***c*** makes a 'sh' sound.

8 *Answers* has a silent ***w***.

9 Most words ending in silent ***e*** keep the ***e*** if the suffix starts with a consonant, e.g. *large, larger, largest, largely*.

10 Nouns ending with 'lf' or 'fe' and some that end in ***f*** change ***f*** to ***v*** to form plurals, e.g. *wolf → wolves, shelf → shelves, half → halves, leaf → leaves* but **not** *roof → roofs, chef → chefs.*

11 Nouns ending in ***s*** form plurals by adding 'es', e.g. *bus → buses, dress → dresses.*

12 Remember how to spell *pieces* by thinking of a *piece* of *pie*.

13 Keep the silent ***e*** to add ***d*** (scare → scared) but drop the ***e*** in *scary, scarier* and *scariest*.

14 Many words for occupations end in 'or', e.g. *author, chiropractor, doctor, visitor, terminator* and *conductor.*

15 *Frightened* has a silent 'gh'. *Fright* rhymes with *night, right, light, sight* and *delight.*

16 *Exciting* has a soft ***c*** because the ***c*** is followed by ***i***. The final ***e*** is dropped to add suffixes: *excited, exciting, excitable*.

17 In *worry* the ***o*** makes a short ***u*** sound found also in *money, monkey, honey, love* and *done.*

18 *Know* has a silent ***k*** as in *knight, knuckle, knee, knew* and *knowledge*.

Standard level questions

GRAMMAR Mini Test 1

Pages 11–12

1 B **2** D **3** A **4** D **5** B **6** B **7** B **8** D **9** C **10** C **11** A **12** A **13** C **14** D **15** B **16** A **17** C **18** D

1 The only pronoun that is accurate is *me.* The writer refers to himself or herself as *me*.

2 The writer is referring to a particular dentist and not dentists in general so the article *the* is needed.

3 The pronoun *I* needs a singular verb *ran.*

4 The only suitable pronoun is *it.* All the others refer to people, not dogs.

5 The preposition *on* tells where to find the apple.

6 *Black* describes the colour of the dog. *Black* is an adjective.

7 Nouns name people, places, animals and things. The noun in this sentence is a thing: an *apple*. It is a common noun because it is an everyday thing. It is described using the adjective *crunchy*.

8 *Lazy* is an adjective. It describes the cat.

9 Every sentence must have a verb or doing word and make sense or be a complete idea.

10 The plural present-tense verb *are* matches the plural noun *bees*. The text is in present tense: *Bees are insects.*

11 The preposition *of* is needed. The other prepositions don't make sense in this sentence.

12 *Make* is the action verb that makes sense.

13 Many questions start with the question words *who, what, where, when, how* and *why.* They can also start with verbs *did* and *is. Is the cat hungry* is a question. It begins with the word *is*.

14 Some adverbs add meaning to verbs and tell **how**. These kinds of adverbs often end with 'ly'. *Quietly* tells **how** to talk.

15 *Mum and I* are two people so the plural verb *are* is needed. *I* is needed because *Mum and I* are the subject of the sentence. It is also polite in English to refer to others before yourself: *Mum and I .... Bill and I ... Pass the rope to Bill and me.*

16 Plural nouns are used for more than one of anything. *Men* is the plural of *man*.

17 A command tells someone to do something. A, B and D are statements. The only command is *Be careful with the scissors*.

18 *Small* and *little* are synonyms. They have a similar meaning.

Intermediate level questions

GRAMMAR Mini Test 2

Pages 13–14

1 B **2** D **3** B **4** A **5** D **6** D **7** C **8** D **9** D **10** B **11** C **12** D **13** C **14** B **15** C **16** D **17** B **18** C

1 The cat is identified as male in the noun group *his foot*. The correct pronoun is *him*.

2 The noun in this sentence is an animal: a *cat*.

3 A verb is needed in this sentence. The only verbs that are options are *flew* and *flying* but *flying* needs another verb to help it (e.g. is flying) so *flew* is the correct choice. A flock *flew*. The verb is in the past tense.

4 *Dad and I* is a noun group consisting of two people, including the writer, *I*. Two people need a plural pronoun *we*.

5 *Said* is a past-tense verb for what the mother duck did (she spoke).

6 *Quickly* is an adverb that tells how.

7 The article *a* is used before nouns that start with consonant sounds. *Monkey* is the only noun that starts with a consonant sound (m).

8 The describing word (adjective) for the cake is *delicious*. The other words are not adjectives.

9 A sentence needs to make sense on its own and it must have a verb or verb group. Option D uses the verb group *was looking*. Note that Option B has a verb (ran) but does not make sense on its own because it has no subject.

10 The way to remember which pronouns to use is to separate them and say, *<u>Dad</u> washed the car. <u>I</u> washed the car. <u>Dad and I</u> washed the car. I* is needed because *Dad and I* are the subject of the sentence. It's polite to name the other person ahead of yourself.

11 The text is a recount. The past-tense verb is *looked* which matches the singular pronoun *it*.

12 *When* is a connecting word. It connects two ideas: *It looked really nice* and *we had finished*.

13 *Can you see the bee* is the only question. It starts with the verb *can*.

14 The action in the sentence is *wash*. *Properly* tells **how** to wash. *Properly* is an adverb. Adverbs add meaning to verbs.

15 In a two-people noun group always refer to the other person ahead of yourself so *Ben and I* is the correct sequence. *Ben and I* are two people so they need a plural verb *are*. *I* is needed because *Ben and I* are the subject of the sentence. You would not say 'Me is in the soccer team'.

16 *Kicked* is the past-tense verb needed.

17 B is not a command. It is a statement. Commands usually start with verbs. A, C and D start with verbs. They are commands.

18 *Exciting* and *thrilling* are synonyms. They have similar meanings so can be used in the sentence without changing the meaning.

GRAMMAR Mini Test 3

Pages 15–16

1 D **2** C **3** B **4** D **5** D **6** A **7** D **8** A **9** A **10** D **11** B **12** A **13** A **14** D **15** D **16** C **17** A **18** C

1 *Under* is a preposition. Prepositions are **position** words. They tell **where** such as *<u>under</u> the umbrella. In, above* and *over* would not make sense in the sentence.

2 *Me* is the personal pronoun that is needed to match *<u>my</u> uniform* in the sentence.

3 *Had* is the verb that matches the subject *Kelly* and the time *this morning*.

4 *They* is the pronoun that can refer to *Ryan and Lara*.

5 *So* is a connecting word that links ideas through reason or cause. The other connecting words (but, although, because) do not make sense in this sentence.

6 *Caught* is the action verb. It is what Paula did with the ball.

7 *Heard* is incorrect in sentence D. It does not

match with the word *could*. The sentence needs to say *I could hear the rain and thunder.*

8 The storm is described as *wild*. *Wild* is the only adjective.

9 Only Option A contains a verb, *was*. A sentence must have a verb and be a complete idea.

10 *Has* is the having verb that matches the noun, *Gia*.

11 *Is* is the verb that matches the pronoun, *her*.

12 *Very* is used to add intensity to words such as *much*. It can't be used with *most* or *really*. *Many* is a number or quantity word and does not make sense in this sentence.

13 *Wear a bike helmet* is a command. Options B, C and D are statements. Commands usually start with verbs, telling what to do.

14 *Gently* tells **how** to pat the tiny kitten. *Gently* is an adverb.

15 *Much* is used for an amount of *glue*.

16 *It* is a pronoun used to refer to a single noun, *glass*.

17 The pronoun *They* refers to *wombats* in the first sentence.

18 The noun in this sentence is a thing: *lunch*.

Advanced level questions

GRAMMAR Mini Test 4

Pages 17–18

1 B 2 C 3 A 4 D 5 C 6 D 7 C 8 A 9 C 10 A
11 C 12 D 13 A 14 D 15 A 16 D 17 C 18 D

1 The noun in this sentence is an animal: a *bird*. The verb *chirped* tells what the bird does. *Loudly* tells how it chirped.

2 *Me* is the pronoun that relates to the writer, *I*. The writing is in the first person.

3 The past-tense verb *cooked* is needed because the event happened *last night*.

4 The pronoun used by *Luis and Mario* to refer to themselves is *us*.

5 *Because* connects through reason or cause and effect.

6 The action is *chewed*. This is what Hugo did.

7 The verb *run* in the sentence 'The cockroach run away quickly' is incorrect. It is the wrong tense. The verb should be *ran*.

8 *Sneaky* is an adjective used to describe the gecko.

9 *Was* is the only verb in the four options. A sentence must have a verb.

10 *Went* is the past-tense verb needed.

11 *We* relates to *I* and *my family* in the first sentence.

12 *Of* is the preposition that makes sense in the sentence.

13 *Do your homework* is a command. It starts with a verb. Option B is a question. Options C and D are statements.

14 *Carefully* is an adverb that tells **how** to stir the soup.

15 To work out which pronoun to use, split the sentence into two: *Mum likes to surf* and *I like to surf*. *I* is needed as *Mum and I* are the subject of the sentence.

16 *Cow* is a singular noun. *Mice* is plural. *Sheep* and *fish* can be singular or plural nouns.

17 *Where are you going?* Options A, B, D need *were*.

18 *A* is the article to use before a word that starts with a consonant sound: *sandcastle(s)*.

GRAMMAR Mini Test 5

Pages 19–20

1 D 2 C 3 D 4 C 5 C 6 B 7 B 8 C 9 A 10 B
11 A 12 C 13 D 14 C 15 D 16 C 17 B 18 A

1 The noun in this sentence is a place: *library*.

2 *Children* is a plural noun so the verb group that matches is *are eating*.

3 *So* is a connecting word. It links ideas through reason or cause and effect.

4 *I've been waiting a long time because Mum is running late* is correct. *Because* is a connective. It links ideas through reason or cause and effect.

5 Action verbs are doing words. In this sentence *snapped* is the action verb.

6 The verb is incorrect in Option B. *Strolled* is a past-tense verb and the event is not in the past. The sentence should read: *It waits for dinner to stroll by*.

7 *Large* is the describing word (adjective) that tells the size of the spider.

8 *Adult saltwater crocodiles will eat anything* is a sentence. It includes the verb group *will eat* and is a complete idea.

Year 2 Literacy Mini Test Answers

9 *Slowly* is an adverb. It tells **how** to mix the eggs and flour.

10 *Lives* is the verb that matches the singular noun, *octopus*.

11 *Under* is a preposition in the sentence. It is the only word that makes sense in the text. An octopus would not hide *over, through* or *beside* shells.

12 *Has* is the verb that matches the pronoun *it*.

13 *When* connects the ideas and makes sense in the text.

14 *It* is the pronoun that refers to the octopus.

15 *Them* refers to *Paco and Emily*.

16 *Flock* is a collective noun. Collective nouns are singular. *Flock* needs a singular verb *is*.

17 *Why were you late?* Options A and D need *Where*. Option C needs *We're* (We are).

18 *Their, there* and *they're* are homophones. They sound the same but have different meanings and are spelt differently. *Their* relates to the noun *children* and can be used in the noun group *their work*.

Standard level questions

PUNCTUATION Mini Test 1

Pages 21–22

1 B 2 D 3 B 4 D 5 C 6 A 7 B 8 D 9 D 10 A
11 A 12 D 13 B 14 A 15 B 16 D 17 B 18 B

1 This sentence is a statement so it should start with a capital letter and end in a full stop.

2 People's names are proper nouns. A proper noun starts with a capital letter (Ella). The statement ends with a full stop.

3 *China* is a proper noun. It is the name of a country and needs a capital letter. The statement starts with a capital letter and ends in a full stop.

4 This is a sentence. It should start with a capital letter and end in a full stop.

5 *James* is a person's name. It is a proper noun and needs a capital letter. The other words are common nouns.

6 *I* is a pronoun that always needs a capital letter. *I* starts the sentence. *Cooma* is a place name proper noun. The sentence needs a full stop at the end.

7 *Australia* is the name of a country. It is a proper noun and needs a capital letter.

8 *Milly* is the proper noun name of a person so *Milly* needs a capital letter.

9 The sentence should end with a full stop.

10 *Do you have a pencil?* is a question. It ends with a question mark.

11 *Run* is *shouted* as a command so it needs an exclamation mark: "*Run!*"

12 This is a statement and needs a full stop at the end.

13 *Greg* is a person's name. It is a proper noun and needs a capital letter.

14 *How* is a question word. The question needs to end in a question mark.

15 *Africa* is the name of a country. It is a proper noun and needs a capital letter.

16 This is a statement of fact. It starts with a capital letter and ends in a full stop. February is the proper noun name of a month of the year while *birthday* is a common noun so does not need a capital letter.

17 The statement should end in a full stop.

18 This is a statement and so should end in a full stop. *Sunday* is a proper noun for the name of a day of the week and so begins with a capital letter.

Intermediate level questions

PUNCTUATION Mini Test 2

Pages 23–24

1 B 2 C 3 A 4 A 5 D 6 A 7 C 8 B 9 B 10 A
11 D 12 D 13 B 14 A 15 A 16 C 17 B 18 C

1 This is a statement. *Holly* starts the statement so needs a capital letter. It is also a proper noun. The statement needs a full stop at the end.

2 The word *teacher* is a common noun so does not need a capital letter. The statement starts with a capital letter and needs a full stop at the end. Quotation marks are not needed.

3 This is a statement and so should end in a full stop. *José* is a person's name and it starts the sentence so it has a capital letter.

4 The statement starts with a capital letter and ends in a full stop.

5 The statement ends in a full stop.

6 *Monday* is a proper noun name of a day of the week. It starts with a capital letter. The statement needs to end with a full stop.

7 This is a statement and needs to end with a full stop.

8 *I am* can be shortened to *I'm*. The apostrophe (') marks the place of the letter that has been left out: *a*.

9 A list of items needs commas to separate the items. There is no comma before *and*.

10 This is a question. It needs to end with a question mark.

11 *Stop!* is an exclamation. It is a single shouted word of warning.

12 *What's the time?* is a question and needs to end with a question mark.

13 *December* is the name of a month. Names of months are proper nouns and need to begin with a capital letter.

14 The question is *Where is the dog?* It should end with a question mark. *Where* is a common question word.

15 This is a statement. It should start with a capital letter and end in a full stop. Tuesday is a name of a day of the week and so is a proper noun. It needs to begin with a capital letter.

16 The proper noun name *Arthur's* starts the statement and has an apostrophe before the ***s*** to show ownership or possession of the birthday. *February* is the proper noun name for a month of the year and so should also begin with a capital letter. The statement should end in a full stop.

17 *April* is the proper noun name for a month. The statement of fact should end in a full stop.

18 A comma is needed to separate each item in a list. No comma is needed before or after *and*.

PUNCTUATION Mini Test 3

Pages 25–26

1 B **2** C **3** C **4** B **5** B **6** C **7** D **8** C **9** C **10** A
11 A **12** C **13** A **14** A **15** D **16** C **17** A **18** B

1 This is a statement and so should start with a capital letter and end in a full stop. The word *teacher* is a common noun and does not need a capital letter.

2 The statement starts with a capital letter and should end in a full stop. *Ms Fong* is the proper noun name of a person and needs capital letters.

3 *"HELP!"* is in capital letters to show that it is screamed loudly. When words are stated loudly or in surprise they are exclamations. Exclamations need exclamation marks (!).

4 The sentence makes a statement. A statement ends in a full stop. No commas are needed in this statement.

5 The sentence makes a statement. Statements start with a capital letter and end in a full stop. Commas are used to separate items in a list: *bread, milk, bananas*. No comma is required before *and*.

6 The sentence makes a statement. Statements start with a capital letter and end in a full stop. *Olivia, Rose, Street* and *Belrose* are proper noun names and need capital letters.

7 The sentence is a statement. Statements end in a full stop.

8 A sentence must have a verb and make sense. *Wear* is the verb in the first sentence. *Won't get* is the verb group in the second sentence.

9 A comma is needed between *flour* and *eggs* to separate the two items in the list.

10 The sentence is a question. It begins with a question word, *what*. Questions often begin with *who, what, where, when, how* and *why*. A question needs to end in a question mark.

11 *Wait!* is an exclamation. The exclamation mark goes inside the speech marks because it relates to the speech.

12 This is a question. It needs a question mark at the end.

13 *Canberra* is the proper noun name of a place. It needs a capital letter. *Mother, father* and *brother* are common nouns. They only need capital letters when they start a sentence or if they are used as names to address someone, e.g. "*Hello, Mother*."

14 This is a question and should end with a question mark. *Is* is a verb that can start a question. Other verbs that can be used to question include *will, does* and *can*.

15 This is a question. It begins with a common question word, *where*. A question is a sentence. It starts with a capital letter and ends with a question mark.

16 *Sunil* is a proper noun name of a person as well as starting the sentence so it needs a

capital letter. The sentence makes a statement so it needs to end in a full stop. *Ten* is a number adjective in this sentence in the noun group *ten years old*. Number adjectives do not need capital letters.

17 *January* is a proper noun name for a month of the year. The statement needs a full stop at the end.

18 Every sentence needs a verb. The verbs in this text are *slept* and *were*. The first sentence is a simple sentence: *We slept in tents*. The second sentence is *Our sleeping bags were snug and warm*. The full stop belongs after the word *tents*.

Advanced level questions

PUNCTUATION Mini Test 4

Pages 27–28

1 B **2** A **3** D **4** C **5** A **6** B **7** B **8** A **9** B **10** A
11 A **12** B **13** A **14** B **15** C **16** D **17** C **18** A

1 This is a statement and so needs to end in a full stop. *Julie Vivas* is the proper noun name of a person so it needs capital letters.

2 This is a statement and so needs to start with a capital letter and end in a full stop. Each word in the book title is a part of a person's name so each word needs to begin with a capital letter.

3 This is a statement and so should start with a capital letter and end in a full stop. *Wednesday* is the proper noun name for a day of the week. It needs to begin with a capital letter.

4 This is a statement and so should begin with a capital letter and end in a full stop. There is no direct speech in the sentence so no speech marks are needed.

5 The statement starts with a capital letter and ends with a full stop. There are three items that the child has been told to do. The first two items need to be separated by a comma: *tidy my room, make my bed*. The third item starts with *and* so it does not need a comma before it. There is no direct speech so no speech marks are needed.

6 *Katie* and *Victoria* are proper noun names so need to begin with capital letters. *Katie* is also the beginning of the sentence. The sentence is a statement and so should end in a full stop.

7 Each sentence needs a verb. The verbs are action verbs, *go* and *catch*. Sentences must make sense. The full stop goes before the word with the capital letter which begins the second sentence, *They*.

8 *I love it!* is an exclamation. It is a short sentence that can be said with emotion. The other sentences are questions.

9 Commas separate items in a list of three or more things. In this sentence the comma separates *strawberries* and *raspberries*. No comma is needed before *and*.

10 This is a question and so should end in a question mark.

11 The warning is shouted so it is an exclamation. The exclamation mark goes inside the speech marks.

12 The sentence is a statement and so should end in a full stop. The word *dinner* is a common noun. It does not need a capital letter.

13 *Sally* is a proper noun. It is the name of a person so it needs to begin with a capital letter.

14 *Why were you late?* is a question and so should end with a question mark. It begins with a common question word, *why*. Other common question words are *who, what, where, when* and *how*. The other sentences are statements.

15 *Boris, Natalie* and *June* are proper nouns. They need to begin with capital letters. The statement needs to start with a capital letter and end with a full stop.

16 *Sydney* is the name of a place. It is a proper noun and needs to begin with a capital letter. The statement should start with a capital letter and end in a full stop.

17 Book titles are proper nouns. They need capital letters.

18 This is a question and needs to end in a question mark. It begins with a common question word, *Who*. Other common question words are *what, where, when, how* and *why*.

PUNCTUATION Mini Test 5

Pages 29–30

1 C **2** D **3** A **4** C **5** D **6** A **7** C **8** A **9** C **10** A
11 D **12** B **13** D **14** B **15** D **16** B **17** D **18** A

1 *Paul Jennings* is a proper noun name of a person. The name needs capital letters. The word *author* is a common noun and so should not begin with a capital letter. The statement should end in a full stop.

2 *Jack* is a proper noun name which needs to begin with a capital letter. The word *dogs* is a common noun and needs no capital letter. The sentence starts with a capital letter and should end in a full stop.

3 The sentence is a question and needs to end with a question mark. *Christine* is a proper noun and needs to begin with a capital letter.

4 The sentence is a statement so it needs to start with a capital letter and end in a full stop. *Moustache* is the cat's name and so needs to begin with a capital letter. *French* is the proper noun name for the language of France.

5 The statement needs to start with a capital letter and end in a full stop. The name of the day is *Monday* which needs to begin with a capital letter.

6 The sentence is a statement and needs a capital letter at the beginning and a full stop at the end. *Indira* is a proper noun name for a person. *India* is a proper noun name of a place.

7 *We* starts the second sentence and needs a capital letter.

8 The direct speech is a question. The question mark goes inside the speech marks after the last word in the question.

9 Commas belong between items in a list of three or more things: *mince, onion and an egg*. Commas are not usually used before *and*.

10 The sentence asks a question so it needs to end with a question mark. The word *opinion* is a common noun and does not need a capital letter.

11 The text is a sentence and needs a full stop rather than an exclamation mark at the end, and final speech marks to enclose what was actually spoken.

12 This is a statement so it needs to finish with a full stop. The word *sandwiches* is a common noun.

13 *Sunday* is the proper noun name for a day of the week. It needs to begin with a capital letter.

14 *I went to the shop. Todd came too*. These are two sentences. Each sentence has a verb and makes sense on its own. The verbs are *went* and *came*.

15 *July* is a proper noun name for a month of the year and so should begin with a capital letter. The statement needs to start with a capital letter and end with a full stop. *It's* is a contraction for *it is* so needs an apostrophe: *it's*.

16 *When* is commonly used to start questions. The question needs a question mark at the end.

17 The two sentences are: *Harry read a book called* The Little Refugee. *I read it too*. The same verb is used in each sentence: *read*.

18 A comma is needed between *cheese* and *tomato* to separate the items in the list. Do not use a comma before *and*.

Standard level questions

READING Mini Test 1: Poster

Page 31

Go to the **inside back cover** for a guide to question types.

1 C **2** D **3** C **4** see below **5** B **6** B

1 This is a **fact-finding type of question**. The answer is a fact in the text. You read *Answers to name Scooter* (see line 4).

2 This is a **fact-finding type of question**. The answer is a fact in the text. You read *Much loved family pet* (see line 10).

3 This is a **fact-finding type of question**. The answer is a fact in the text. You read *He barks on 'talk' command* (see line 9).

4 This is a **fact-finding type of question**. The noun groups (descriptive adjective and noun) are in the text: *White [dog]* (line 3); *Short hair* (line 6); *tan ears* (line 3); *blue collar* (line 8).

5 This is an **inferring type of question**. To work out the answer you have to 'read between the lines'. You read the dog is a *Much loved family pet* (see line 10) and that *Children are very upset* (see line 11). You can work out that the family is feeling sad about losing its pet.

6 This is a **judgement type of question**. You read the title of the poster *Lost Dog* (see line 1). You also read *Reward $100* (see line 13). Rewards are offered to encourage people to find something. In this case you can work out that the purpose of the poster is to help the family find the lost dog.

READING Mini Test 2: Advertisement

Page 32

1 A **2** C **3** B **4** B **5** D **6** C, F

1 This is a **fact-finding type of question**. The answer is a fact in the text. You read *A yummy new sweet treat for the whole family* (see line 3).

2 This is a **synthesis type of question**. To work out the answer you have to read the whole text. You read all the advantages of Blue Chompees such as *yummy new sweet treat* (see line 3), *packed with energy* (see line 5), *No artificial flavours* (see line 9). Use your understanding of persuasive text to recognise that the advertisement wants you to buy Blue Chompees.

3 This is an **inferring type of question**. To work out the answer you have to 'read between the lines'. You read *Have some every day* (see line 8) to encourage you to buy more. In this way the makers of Blue Chompees make more money.

4 This is a **fact-finding type of question**. The answer is a fact in the text. You read *sweet treat for the whole family* (see line 3) and *Share them with friends* (see line 8).

5 This is a **fact-finding type of question**. The answer is a fact in the text. You read *AVAILABLE NOW in shops everywhere* (see lines 10–11).

6 This is a **judgement type of question**. You should judge that the Chompees must be blue because of their name (see lines 1–2). The purpose of the advertisement is to make you think the Chompees are good for you because they give you energy (see line 6) and vitamin C (see line 10) but you should judge Chompees to be unhealthy because they are made of sugar (line 6).

Intermediate level questions

READING Mini Test 3: Recount

Page 33

1 A **2** D **3** C **4** A **5** B **6** D

1 This is a **fact-finding type of question**. The answer is a fact in the text. You read *a vet took some X-rays. Luckily the joey had no broken bones* (see lines 7–8).

2 This is a **fact-finding type of question**. The answer is a fact in the text. You read *The mother kangaroo had been killed by a car* (see lines 3–4).

3 This is a **fact-finding type of question**. The answer is a fact in the text. You read *My aunt looks after native animals that have been hurt* (see line 2).

4 This is a **fact-finding type of question**. The answer is a fact in the text. You read *She had to feed it every four hours* (see lines 9–10).

5 This is a **fact-finding type of question**. The answer is a fact in the text. You read *it went to live in a paddock at the sanctuary* (see lines 13–14).

6 This is a **fact-finding type of question**. The answer is a fact in the text. You read *It slept inside a baby's blanket* (see line 11).

READING Mini Test 4: Discussion

Page 34

1 C **2** D **3** B **4** C **5** A **6** C

1 This is a **synthesis type of question**. To work out the answer you have to read the whole text and count the number of flightless birds mentioned: *emu, ostrich, cassowary, rhea, kiwi, dodo, penguin (see lines 5, 6, 10, 15, 17, 26, 32)*.

2 This is an **inferring type of question**. To work out the answer you have to 'read between the lines'. You read that *Emus and ostriches can't fly [because t]heir wings are too small and they are too heavy* (see lines 5–9). It also says that *Cassowaries are like emus* (see line 10). You can infer that the reason cassowaries can't fly is the same reason that emus and ostriches can't: *their wings are too small* (see lines 7–8).

3 This is a **judgement type of question**. You read *My nana laughs and calls me a dodo when I'm being silly* (see lines 30–31). You can judge that Josh's nana is making a joke because she laughs.

4 This is a **fact-finding type of question**. The answer is a fact in the text. You read that kiwis are *killed by cats, dogs, ferrets* (see line 24). Kiwis are also killed by cars but a car is not an animal and the question asks *which* ***animals*** *kill kiwis*.

5 This is a **fact-finding type of question**. The answer is a fact in the text. You read that the *rhea* [is] *from South America* (see lines 15–16).

6 This is a **judgement type of question**. You read that students and the teacher contribute ideas to the discussion. You can work out that the class is sharing ideas about flightless birds.

Year 2 Literacy Mini Test Answers

READING Mini Test 5: Poem

Page 35

1 B **2** B **3** B **4** C **5** D **6** C

1 This is a **language type of question**. To work out the answer you have to read the text carefully, especially the last stanza *(see lines 26–33)*. *Swish* is the sound made by the crocodile's tail. *Snap* is the sound made by its jaws. *Crunch* is the sound made when the crocodile bites something. 'Gulp' is not used in the poem.

2 This is a **fact-finding type of question**. The answer is a fact in the text. You read that the crocodile is *a log with yellow eyes (see line 6)*.

3 This is a **language type of question**. To work out the answer you have to read the text carefully, especially the section that is quoted: the crocodile was *baking in the sun (see line 13)*. This means that it was sunbaking.

4 This is a **language type of question**. To work out the answer you have to read the text carefully, especially the section that is quoted: the poet warns the reader *don't be fooled (see line 23)*. The other answers are not warnings for the reader but descriptions of the crocodile.

5 This is a **synthesis type of question**. To work out the answer you have to read the whole text. You read *Tricky things those crocodiles (see lines 18–19)*. You also read *don't be fooled (see line 23)*. The poet thinks crocodiles are tricky.

6 This is a **judgement type of question**. You read *They can move quickly (see line 26)*. None of the other options appear in the poem.

READING Mini Test 6: Narrative

Page 36

1 A **2** C **3** D **4** D **5** B **6** C

1 This is a **fact-finding type of question**. The answer is a fact in the text. You read *Luca was shocked (see line 2)*.

2 This is an **inferring type of question**. The answer can be inferred in the text. You read *Lisa put the chocolate bar in her pocket and walk[ed] out of the shop. She didn't pay for it! (see lines 2–4)*. You can infer she stole it.

3 This is an **inferring type of question**. To work out the answer you have to 'read between the lines'. You read that Luca says *"I don't want any. It's not right." (see line 16)*. The chocolate is stolen. The text says that Luca is shocked about this. You can infer that he won't eat something that wasn't paid for.

4 This is a **fact-finding type of question**. The answer is a fact in the text. You read *He decided to tell his mother (see lines 31–32)*.

5 This is a **synthesis type of question**. After reading the whole text readers will understand that Luca is concerned about Lisa. She is his friend and he likes her. He already knows it's wrong to steal things so he does not need to ask answer D. He will say to his mother that Lisa stole from a shop.

6 This is a **fact-finding type of question**. The answer is a fact in the text. You read *If he told his mother maybe she could talk with Lisa's mother (see lines 24–25)*.

Advanced level questions

READING Mini Test 7: Playscript

Pages 37–38

1 A **2** C **3** B **4** D **5** D **6** C

1 This is a **language type of question**. To work out the answer you have to read the text carefully, especially the section that is quoted: *How did the intruder get in? (see line 7)*. You also read that *our house had been broken into (see lines 3–4)*. The intruder in the playscript had broken into the house while the bears were out so *intruder* means 'someone who comes onto your property without permission'.

2 This is a **fact-finding type of question**. The answer is a fact in the text. You read that the bears *found someone asleep in Baby Bear's bed (see line 5)*.

3 This is a **language type of question**. To work out the answer you have to read the text carefully, especially the section that is quoted: *When she ran off, in which direction did she travel? (see line 11)*. The bears then described which way she went. You can work out that the question meant 'which way did she go?'

4 This is a **language type of question**. To work out the answer you have to read the text carefully, especially the section that is quoted: *She ran left down our street and turned right onto Briar Lane. We lost sight of her after that*

(see lines 12–13). The word *that* refers to [she] *turned right onto Briar Lane*.

5 This is a **fact-finding type of question**. The answer is a fact in the text. You read *She had on a red hoodie and dark blue pants (see lines 18–19)*. You also read *a running girl with long curly yellow hair (see lines 26–27)*. The full description of the intruder includes what she is wearing. All suggestions are partially correct but only D gives the full description.

6 This is a **language type of question**. To work out the answer you have to read the text carefully, especially the section that is quoted: *Baby Bear (sobbing) (see line 6)*. *Sobbing* means 'crying'. This is the only option that describes a feeling of upset.

READING Mini Test 8: Report

Pages 39–40

1 C **2** [1, 4, 3, 2] **3** **A** false **B** true **C** true **D** true **E** true **4** C **5** A **6** C

1 This is a **fact-finding type of question**. The answer is a fact in the text. You read *They make nests using chewed-up wood and plant stems, mixed with saliva (see lines 5–6)*.

2 This is a **synthesis type of question**. To work out the answer you have to read the whole text. Paragraph three describes the life cycle of the paper wasp so you need to read the text carefully and then summarise the life cycle sequence for yourself.

3 This is a **fact-finding type of question**. The true answers B, C, D and E are facts in the text. A is false because the paper wasp larvae (not the adults) eat chewed-up insects.

4 This is a **fact-finding type of question**. The answer is a fact in the text. You read *The queen wasp lays all the eggs in the nest (see line 8)*.

5 This is an **inferring type of question**. The answer can be inferred from the text. You read that paper wasps *kill insects such as caterpillars. Caterpillars can destroy gardens (see lines 12–13)*. You can infer from this that gardeners should like the paper wasps.

6 This is a **fact-finding type of question**. The answer is a fact in the text. You read that *Paper wasps will attack humans who disturb their nest (see line 15)*.

READING Mini Test 9: Description

Page 41

1 A **2** C **3** B **4** D **5** B **6** C

1 This is a **judgement type of question**. You read *a best friend is someone you enjoy being with … Sasha is my best friend (see lines 13–14)*. From this you can work out that the writer enjoys Sasha's company.

2 This is a **fact-finding type of question**. The answer is a fact in the text. You read *he can be a bit cheeky in class. Then he gets into trouble (see line 3)*.

3 This is a **fact-finding type of question**. The answer is a fact in the text. You read *He was born with a disability. He can't walk or run (see line 5)*.

4 This is a **fact-finding type of question**. The answer is a fact in the text. You read *Sasha says one day he is going to compete in the Paralympics … I think he will play wheelchair basketball (see lines 10–12)*.

5 This is a **fact-finding type of question**. The answer is a fact in the text. You read *Sometimes we are a bit careless with our bags … Then Sasha gets angry with us (see lines 8–9)*.

6 This is a **synthesis type of question**. To work out the answer you have to read the whole text. The title of the text is *My best friend (see line 1)* and the whole passage is a description of the author's best friend. The last paragraph gives the author's opinion on friendship. From this you can work out the text is about friendship, more than any of the other suggestions.

READING Mini Test 10: Explanation

Pages 42–43

1 [2, 4, 1, 3] **2** D **3** D **4** D **5** A **6** B

1 This is a **synthesis type of question**. To work out the answer you have to read the whole text. Paragraph one has the information needed.

2 This is a **fact-finding type of question**. The answer is a fact in the text. You read *The blood carries the oxygen (see line 4)*. You also read *If the brain stops getting oxygen, it has a brain attack. This is called a stroke (see lines 13–15)*.

3 This is a **fact-finding type of question**. The answer is a fact in the text. You read *Puffing,*

panting and deep breathing help to get more oxygen into our lungs (see lines 9–10).

4 This is a **fact-finding type of question**. The answer is a fact in the text. You read *Our brain needs more oxygen than any other part of us* (see lines 12–13).

5 This is a **fact-finding type of question**. The answer is a fact in the text. You read *when we are exercising we need much more oxygen* (see line 7).

6 This is a **synthesis type of question**. To work out the answer you have to read the whole text. You read the title is *Oxygen* (see line 1). The whole text is about how our bodies use oxygen.

WRITING Mini Test 1: Persuasive text

Page 46

Marking checklist for a persuasive text

Read the text. Gather an overall impression first, then read the text a second time to consider each of the ten assessment criteria below. Tick each correct point.

Audience

- ☐ Does the text engage an audience?
- ☐ Does the text meet the needs of an audience?

Text structure

- ☐ Is there a heading to orient the reader?
- ☐ Does the text have an introduction, body and conclusion/recommendation?
- ☐ Does the writer make strong claims?
- ☐ Are there reasons and elaboration?
- ☐ Is there a call to action?

Ideas

- ☐ Are the ideas well thought through?
- ☐ Does the writing show originality or creativity?
- ☐ Are the arguments supported by facts?
- ☐ Does the text reflect an understanding of real-life persuasive texts?

Persuasive devices

- ☐ Does the writer persuade though logic or exaggeration?
- ☐ Does the writer address the reader directly (*you*)?
- ☐ Does the writer use emotive language?
- ☐ Does the text include high modality statements (e.g. *It is wrong.*)?
- ☐ Are auxiliary verbs and modal adverbs used (e.g. *must*, *should*, *absolutely*, *definitely*)?

Vocabulary

- ☐ Are there technical terms?
- ☐ Are noun groups used effectively?
- ☐ Are a range of adjectives (e.g. *fantastic*, *useless*, *dreadful*)

Cohesion

- ☐ Are reference chains consistent (e.g. *people—they*)?
- ☐ Are arguments linked logically using connectives (e.g. *therefore*, *because*, *so*)?
- ☐ Is repetition used for emphasis or reinforcement?

Paragraphing

- ☐ Are paragraphs sequenced logically?
- ☐ Is each paragraph based on a main idea with supporting detail?

Sentence structure

- ☐ Are sentences grammatically correct and meaningful?
- ☐ Is there evidence of a range of sentence types, as appropriate?
- ☐ Is sentence length varied for pace and emphasis, if appropriate?

Punctuation

- ☐ Is punctuation accurate for sentence beginnings and endings, proper nouns, contractions, exclamations and direct speech?

Spelling

- ☐ Is the spelling accurate?
- ☐ Have attempts been made to spell unknown words?
- ☐ Are the attempts phonetically correct or readable?
- ☐ Do the writer's spelling attempts demonstrate understanding of various aspects of spelling?
- ☐ Does the student spell simple, common, difficult and challenging words correctly?

Writing samples

Go to **pages 117–118** for Intermediate and Advanced Writing samples for Mini Test 1.

WRITING Mini Test 2: Narrative text

Page 47

Marking checklist for a narrative text

Read the text. Gather an overall impression first, then read the text a second time to consider the ten assessment criteria. Tick each correct point.

Audience

- ☐ Is the text interesting and entertaining?
- ☐ Does the action in the plot draw the reader in?
- ☐ Does the story make sense?
- ☐ Can you form a mental picture of the characters and setting?

Text structure

- ☐ Does the text have an appropriate structure?
- ☐ Is there an orientation, complication, series of events, climax and resolution?
- ☐ Is the resolution satisfying for a reader?

Ideas

- ☐ Does the story show understanding of the relevant genre (fantasy, mystery, science fiction, realism, adventure)?
- ☐ Are the ideas logical, original and imaginative?
- ☐ Are the ideas thought through?
- ☐ Is there enough detail?
- ☐ Is the writer able to write convincingly about the subject?

Character and setting

- ☐ Are the characters well rounded?
- ☐ Is the point of view of characters evident?
- ☐ Can a reader feel empathy with the characters?
- ☐ Is the setting credible and well described?

Vocabulary

- ☐ Are noun groups (nouns and adjectives) used effectively?
- ☐ Are verbs used appropriately to describe the characters' actions and behaviour?
- ☐ Is verb tense accurate and consistent?
- ☐ Are adverbs used appropriately?
- ☐ Does the writer make use of figurative language (simile, alliteration, metaphor, onomatopoeia)?

Cohesion

- ☐ Is the use of first- or third-person narrator consistent throughout the text?
- ☐ Does the text flow logically?
- ☐ Are connectives used to link ideas?
- ☐ Does the writer use synonyms, antonyms and word sets to create interesting lexical chains?

Paragraphing

- ☐ Are paragraphs used to organise sections of the story?
- ☐ Are paragraphs built around topic sentences?

Sentence structure

- ☐ Are a variety of sentence structures evident, as appropriate (simple, compound, complex; direct and reported speech)?
- ☐ Does the text include statements, commands and exclamations, as appropriate?
- ☐ Is sentence length varied for pace and emphasis?

Punctuation

- ☐ Is sentence punctuation evident and accurate, including direct speech?
- ☐ Are there capital letters for sentence beginnings and proper nouns, such as the names of characters?
- ☐ Are commas and full stops used accurately and consistently?

Spelling

- ☐ Is the spelling accurate?
- ☐ Have attempts been made to spell unknown words?
- ☐ Are the attempts phonetically correct or readable?
- ☐ Do the writer's spelling attempts demonstrate understanding of various aspects of spelling?
- ☐ Does the student spell simple, common, difficult and challenging words correctly?

Writing samples

Go to **pages 119–120** for Intermediate and Advanced Writing samples for Mini Test 2.

WRITING Mini Test 3: Recount text

Page 48

Marking checklist for a recount text

Read the text. Gather an overall impression first, then read the text a second time to consider each of the ten assessment criteria below. Tick each correct point.

Year 2 Literacy Mini Test Answers

Audience

- ☐ Is the text interesting/relevant for its target audience?
- ☐ Does the recount make sense?

Text structure

- ☐ Does the text have an appropriate structure?
- ☐ Does it include an introduction to orient the reader to setting, people and time?
- ☐ Does the body of the text have enough detail?
- ☐ Does it have a concluding statement or summing up, if appropriate?

Ideas

- ☐ Are the ideas sequenced chronologically?
- ☐ Are the ideas thought through?
- ☐ Is the writer able to write with authority about the events?

Character and setting

- ☐ Are the writer's opinions about the event evident?
- ☐ Are people and setting well described?

Vocabulary

- ☐ Is there sufficient detail?
- ☐ Are noun groups (nouns and adjectives) used effectively?
- ☐ Are verbs used appropriately for actions and activity?
- ☐ Are past-tense verbs used consistently?
- ☐ Are pronouns used consistently for a first-person recount?

Cohesion

- ☐ Does the text flow chronologically?
- ☐ Are time connectives used to link ideas (e.g. *then*, *after that*, *meanwhile*)?
- ☐ Are adverbials used to establish time sequence (e.g. *last weekend*, *on Monday*)?
- ☐ Is noun–pronoun reference accurate (e.g. *Mum—she*)?

Paragraphing

- ☐ Are paragraphs used to organise aspects of the topic?
- ☐ Are paragraphs built around topic sentences?

Sentence structure

- ☐ Are a variety of sentence structures evident, as appropriate (simple, compound, complex; direct and indirect speech)?

Punctuation

- ☐ Is sentence punctuation evident and accurate?
- ☐ Are there capital letters for sentence beginnings and proper nouns?
- ☐ Are commas and full stops used accurately and consistently?

Spelling

- ☐ Is the spelling accurate?
- ☐ Have attempts been made to spell unknown words?
- ☐ Are the attempts phonetically correct or readable?
- ☐ Does the student spell simple, common, difficult and challenging words correctly?

Writing samples

Go to **pages 121–122** for Intermediate and Advanced Writing samples for Mini Test 3.

Standard level

CONVENTIONS OF LANGUAGE

Sample Test 1

Pages 50–54

1 C (Standard level) **2 D** (Standard level) **3 B** (Standard level) **4 D** (Standard level) **5 D** (Standard level) **6 C** (Standard level) **7 B** (Intermediate level) **8 A** (Standard level) **9 B** (Intermediate level) **10 D** (Intermediate level) **11 A** (Standard level) **12 C** (Standard level) **13 B** (Standard level) **14 D** (Advanced level) **15 A** (Standard level) **16 C** (Intermediate level) **17 D** (Advanced level) **18 C** (Advanced level) **19 B** (Intermediate level) **20 A** (Intermediate level) **21 D, E** (Standard level) **22 dry clothes; noisy magpies; soft skin; tall tree** (Standard level) **23 Did you eat your banana for lunch?** (Standard level) **24 Common nouns: teacher, place, cat; Proper nouns: Ms Cheung, Tasmania, Mr Whiskers** (Standard level) **25 A a B an C a D an** (Standard level) **26 garden** (Standard level) **27 started** (Standard level) **28 loves** (Standard level) **29 said** (Standard level) **30 Don't** (Standard level) **31 was** (Standard level) **32 stopped** (Standard level) **33 until** (Standard level) **34 likes** (Standard level) **35 are** (Standard level) **36 blue** (Standard level) **37 fur** (Intermediate level) **38 huge** (Advanced level) **39 tail** (Intermediate level) **40 some** (Standard level) **41 gardening** (Intermediate level) **42 unhappy** (Intermediate level) **43 babies** (Intermediate level) **44 taking** (Advanced level) **45 fright** (Advanced level) **46 threw** (Advanced level) **47 your** (Standard level) **48 every** (Standard level) **49 water** (Intermediate level) **50 for** (Standard level)

1 The sentence is about something that has already happened. *Ran* is a past-tense verb.

2 *We* is a personal pronoun. Personal pronouns replace nouns in a text. In this text *we* refers to the noun group *Molly and I*.

3 *Because* is a connecting word (conjunction). It is used to connect ideas through cause and effect. The fact that the dog has an eye infection causes its owners to keep it inside.

4 Pronouns can replace nouns in sentences. The pronoun *herself* refers to *Mum*. Instead of saying *Mum bought Mum new shoes* a pronoun is used so that the word *Mum* does not have to be repeated.

5 The noun is *chair*. Nouns name people, places, animals and things.

6 *Slid* is the action taken by the dog. *Slid* is what the dog did.

7 The describing word is *sweet*. *Sweet* is used to describe the taste of the *strawberries*.

8 *Rode* is the past-tense form of the verb *ride*. 'Rided' is not a word. *Ride* is an irregular verb. Irregular verbs don't use 'ed' to show past tense like regular verbs do (e.g. jump → jumped). Other irregular verbs include *fly* → *flew*, *eat* → *ate*, *write* → *wrote*.

9 *Have* is a helper verb. It forms part of the verb group *have finished*.

10 The action verb is *stir*. The adverb *thoroughly* tells **how** to stir. An adverb adds information about the verb. Adverbs that tell **how** often end with the letters 'ly'.

11 Commands tell you to do something. They usually start with a verb (Tie). They can also start with an adverb (Quickly tie). B is a question. C and D are statements.

12 A sentence that makes a statement starts with a capital letter and ends with a full stop. The word *red* is an adjective and so does not need a capital letter.

13 This sentence is a question. It correctly ends with a question mark. A, C and D are statements and should end with full stops. Questions often begin with words such as *who, what, where, when, how, why,* or verbs such as *will, can, have, is, do*.

14 This is a statement. A statement begins with a capital letter and ends with a full stop. Commas are used to separate items in a list. No comma is needed before *and*.

15 Plural means 'more than one'. Nouns can be singular or plural. The correct spelling is *babies*.

16 *Man* is a singular noun. The plural of *man* is *men*. *Sheep* and *fish* have the same form for singular and plural. *People* is plural for *person*.

17 *Of* is a preposition. Prepositions can indicate substance, e.g. *of pie*, *of cream*, *of apples*.

Year 2 Literacy Sample Online-style Test Answers

Prepositions always belong with nouns. D uses *of* incorrectly. The sentence should be: *He should have shared it with me*. The word *should* needs to be used with a verb such as *have*.

18 It is polite to refer to the other person before yourself in a sentence. The word *I* should be used instead of *me*. To work out whether *me* or *I* should be used separate the sentence into *I like our new teacher* and *Justin likes our new teacher*. You would not say 'Me likes our new teacher'.

19 A statement starts with a capital letter and ends in a full stop. *Heidi, Sally* and *Canberra* are proper nouns. Proper nouns need capital letters.

20 *Children* is a plural noun. The verb must be plural to match it: *children were*.

21 In this question the words *before* and *after* are prepositions that help you determine **when**. The days of the week occur in sequence.

22 Adjectives (*dry*, *noisy*, *soft*, *tall*) are describing words. They can be used to describe people, places, animals and things.

23 A question asks for an answer. A question ends in a question mark.

24 Nouns are words for people, places, animals and things. Proper nouns begin with capital letters because they are names for specific people, places, animals and things.

25 Articles are *a*, *an* and *the*. Use *an* in front of words that commence with a vowel sound (a, e, i, o, u); e.g. *an ugly toad*; *a fat toad*.

26 Try to remember that *garden* ends in the smaller word *den*.

27 *Started* is the word *start* with the suffix 'ed' for past tense.

28 *Loves* is a common word. You need to remember how to spell it. Remember to use ***o***.

29 *Said* sounds like 'sed'. Learn this common word to use in your own writing. Remember that *said* is past tense for the verb *say* and you will remember that *said* and *say* start with 'sa'.

30 *Don't* is a contraction for *do not*. The apostrophe (') marks the place of the missing letter ***o***.

31 *Was* is a common word. You cannot spell it by sounding it out. You just need to remember it.

32 *Stopped* is a past-tense verb. It is the word *stop* with the suffix 'ed'. When adding suffixes to one-syllable words that end in a vowel then a final consonant, you usually need to double the final consonant (e.g. hop → hopped, hit → hitting).

33 *Until* ends in a single ***l***.

34 The silent ***e*** at the end of *like* makes the ***i*** say its own name in the word. Don't confuse it with *licks* which has a short ***i*** sound in the middle.

35 *Are* is a common word. Remember the ***e*** is silent.

36 *Blue* has the vowel pattern 'ue' as in *glue, hue, due* and *pursue*.

37 *Fur* is spelt with 'ur' as in *blur, urgent, further, hurt* and *burn*.

38 *Huge* has a soft ***g*** because the ***g*** is followed by an ***e***. The ***u–e*** combination means that the ***u*** says its own name inside the word. This is a long vowel sound.

39 *Tail* has the 'ai' vowel pattern. This pattern can be found in hail, rail, rain, pain, gain, paint, faint.

40 *Some* means 'an amount of something'. *Sum* means 'to add up'. *Some* and *sum* are homophones. Homophones are words that sound the same but are spelt differently and have different meanings. Remember what *homophone* means by thinking about hearing sounds in a *phone*.

41 *Gardening* is made by adding the suffix 'ing' to *garden*. If you remember the base word is *garden* you will remember the ***e***.

42 *Unhappy* uses a prefix 'un' in front of the word *happy* to make an opposite meaning. Other words which use 'un' are *done* → *undone, do* → *undo, believeable* → *unbelievable, usual* → *unusual.*

43 *Babies* is plural for *baby*. When making plurals of nouns that end in ***y***, change the ***y*** to ***i*** to add 'es' (e.g. lollies, jellies, ponies, puppies).

44 Drop the ***e*** from *take* to add 'ing'.

45 *Fright* has six letters but four sounds. The 'igh' make one long ***i*** sound. It rhymes with *right, light, delight, sight, fight* and *might*.

46 *Threw* is spelt with 'ew' as in *chew, drew, new* and *grew*. It is the past-tense form of the irregular verb *throw*.

47 *Your* begins with *you* with an ***r*** added.

48 *Every* begins with *ever* with a ***y*** added.

49 The ***a*** in water sounds like 'or'. Other words with this sound include *war* and *wardrobe*.

50 There are three words that sound the same but are spelt differently: *four*, *for* and *fore*.

Intermediate level

CONVENTIONS OF LANGUAGE

Sample Test 2

Pages 55–58

1 C (Standard level) **2 A** (Intermediate level) **3 B** (Intermediate level) **4 B** (Intermediate level) **5 B** (Intermediate level) **6 D** (Intermediate level) **7 C** (Standard level) **8 A** (Standard level) **9 B** (Standard level) **10 C** (Standard level) **11 B** (Intermediate level) **12 D** (Advanced level) **13 C** (Intermediate level) **14 A** (Advanced level) **15 D** (Intermediate level) **16 A** (Intermediate level) **17 D** (Advanced level) **18 B** (Intermediate level) **19 C** (Intermediate level) **20 A** (Advanced level) **21 D F** (Standard level) **22 happy baby; icy drink; strong fence; full moon** (Standard level) **23 Line up on the grass.** (Standard level) **24 Common nouns: dog, city, girl; Proper nouns: Emma, German Shepherd, Melbourne** (Standard level) **25 A a B a C a D an** (Standard level) **26 yesterday** (Intermediate level) **27 asked** (Standard level) **28 could** (Intermediate level) **29 talk** (Standard level) **30 pieces** (Advanced level) **31 lamb** (Intermediate level) **32 calf** (Intermediate level) **33 called** (Intermediate level) **34 wouldn't** (Advanced level) **35 footpath** (Intermediate level) **36 chain** (Intermediate level) **37 pineapple** (Advanced level) **38 grapes** (Standard level) **39 tomatoes** (Advanced level) **40 followed** (Intermediate level) **41 answer** (Advanced level) **42 mistake** (Intermediate level) **43 beginning** (Intermediate level) **44 holidays** (Intermediate level) **45 next** (Standard level) **46 teacher** (Standard level) **47 please** (Standard level) **48 friend** (Intermediate level) **49 class** (Standard level) **50 looked** (Standard level)

1 *Fell* is the past-tense form of the verb *fall*. You know to use past tense because *jumped* is in the past tense.

2 *Liam and me* is a noun group that names two people, *Liam* and the writer, *me*, in the first person. *Liam and me* needs to be replaced by the pronoun *us*.

3 The noun is *cat*. Nouns name people, places, animals and things.

4 *Her* is a pronoun that replaces the word *Mum* in the sentence. It would be clumsy to say *Mum asked me to pass Mum the sauce*. So, we replace *Mum* with *her*.

5 Action verbs are doing verbs. The action in this sentence is *ran*.

6 *Yellow* describes the colour of the flowers.

7 People speak *on* the telephone.

8 We talk *to* people (or 'with' people).

9 *Some* is used for an indefinite quantity.

10 The pronoun *he* is singular and needs a singular past-tense verb, *was*, to match.

11 You cannot say *I is*. *Was* is the singular past-tense verb needed.

12 *Before* connects events in time order.

13 *Quickly* tells **how** Kirra ate. *Quickly* is an adverb. Adverbs add information to verbs. Many adverbs end in 'ly'.

14 *Look!* is a single verb command. It is also an exclamation.

15 A statement begins with a capital letter and ends in a full stop. *Perth* is the name of a place so it is a proper noun and needs a capital letter.

16 *What's the time?* is a question and is punctuated correctly. Questions often commence with words such as *who, what, how, when, where, why, can* and *will*. B, C and D are statements and should end in full stops.

17 The sentence has some direct speech which should be included inside speech or quotation marks. Only the words spoken should be inside the speech marks.

18 A sentence needs at least one verb. B is the only suggestion that includes a verb (eat) and is a complete idea.

19 *Katy* is a proper noun and starts with a capital letter. It is also the first word in the sentence. The months of the year are also proper nouns, so *June* needs a capital letter. A statement begins with a capital letter and ends with a full stop.

20 *One* is used to refer to a *book*. It is used instead of the noun *book*: *That book is better than this book*.

21 The days of the week occur in sequence. Prepositions *before* and *after* are used to tell **when** in the sentences.

22 Adjectives are describing words. They describe nouns (people, places, animals and things).

23 A command is a sentence. A sentence begins with a capital letter and end in a full stop, exclamation mark or question mark. A command usually starts with a verb.

24 Proper nouns are names for specific people, places, animals or things. A proper noun begins with a capital letter.

25 Articles are *a*, *an* and *the*. Use *an* in front of words that commence with a vowel sound (a, e, i, o, u); e.g. *an ugly toad*; *a fat toad*.

26 This word has three syllables: *yes–ter–day*. Two of the syllables are actual words. Remember the 'ter' in the middle. Pronounce the word carefully to help work out the spelling.

27 *Asked* is a common word to learn for your own writing. It is a past-tense verb formed by adding 'ed' to *ask*. Rhyming words which include the smaller word *ask* are *task, flask, cask, bask* and *mask*.

28 *Could* rhymes with *should* and *would*. These words have a silent ***l***.

29 *Talk* rhymes with *walk* and *chalk*. The 'al' makes an 'aw' sound.

30 *Pieces* starts with the word *pie*. Remember ***i*** before ***e*** in this word by thinking about a *piece* of *pie*.

31 *Lamb* has a silent ***b*** as in *comb, thumb, crumb* and *dumb*.

32 *Calf* is spelt with 'al' that says 'ah' as in *calm*.

33 *Called* is a past-tense verb made by adding 'ed' to *call*. Other words in the same family include *caller, calling* and *calls*.

34 *Wouldn't* is a contraction of *would not*. The place of the missing ***o*** is marked by the apostrophe as in *couldn't* and *shouldn't*.

35 *Footpath* is a compound word made from *foot + path*. The ***a*** sound in *path* is the same as in *bath, class, pass, daft* and *raft*.

36 *Chain* is spelt with 'ai' that is also found in *pain, rain, train, stain, rail, pail, snail* and *detail*.

37 *Pineapple* is a compound word made of *pine + apple*. Remembering these two words will help you remember the ***e*** in *pine*. *Apple* ends in 'le' as in *settle, rattle, little, table* and *grapple*.

38 *Grapes* is a plural noun. The ***a*** says its own name because the base word *grape* has the ***a–e*** spelling pattern.

39 *Tomatoes* is a plural noun. Words that end in ***o*** usually add 'es' to form plurals, e.g. *volcanoes, potatoes*. Some can be spelt with ***s*** or 'es', e.g. *mangos* or *mangoes*.

40 The past-tense verb *followed* is made by adding the suffix 'ed' to *follow*.

41 *Answer* has a silent ***w***.

42 *Mistake* has only one ***s***.

43 When the syllable at the end of a word has a short vowel and a final consonant ('gin' in *begin*) double the final consonant to add the suffix 'ing': *beginning*.

44 *Holidays* has three syllables: *ho–li–days*. Breaking words into syllables sometimes helps you work out the spelling.

45 *Next* has 'xt' which sounds like it should be spelt 'ckst'. Other words which use 'xt' are *extreme, extinct, extra* and *extend*.

46 *Teacher* ends in 'er'. Many words for occupations end in 'er'; e.g. *dancer, gardener, painter, plumber, fruiterer*.

47 *Please* has the spelling pattern 'ea'. These letters are used in *pea, leap, heap, beam, cream, cheat*.

48 *Friend* has a silent ***i***.

49 *Class* rhymes with *glass, grass, pass*.

50 *Looked* ends in 'ed'. The 'ed' ending is used at the end of many verbs to let readers know the action happened in the past. Compare present tense, past tense and future tense in these sentences: *I am looking now. I looked yesterday. I will look tomorrow.*

Advanced level

CONVENTIONS OF LANGUAGE

Sample Test 3

Pages 59–62

1 B (Standard level) **2 D** (Advanced level) **3 D** (Standard level) **4 C** (Intermediate level) **5 B** (Intermediate level) **6 B** (Standard level) **7 D** (Advanced level) **8 C** (Advanced level) **9 B** (Advanced level) **10 D** (Advanced level) **11 C** (Advanced level) **12 A** (Intermediate level) **13 C** (Advanced level) **14 B** (Standard level) **15 B** (Intermediate level) **16 A** (Intermediate level) **17 D** (Intermediate level) **18 D** (Intermediate level) **19 C** (Intermediate level) **20 A** (Advanced level) **21 C, H** (Intermediate level) **22 Ms Barton—she; Mr Walsh—he; the children—they; the ball—it** (Advanced level) **23 What did you have for breakfast?** (Intermediate level) **24 ran swiftly, laughed loudly, ate greedily, listened carefully** (Advanced level) **25 The hungry tiger** (Advanced level) **26 rare** (Advanced level) **27 tripped** (Intermediate level) **28 scissors** (Advanced level) **29 sunburnt** (Intermediate level) **30 scratching** (Intermediate level) **31 quickly** (Intermediate level) **32 watch** (Intermediate level) **33 sorry** (Standard level) **34 learn** (Advanced level) **35 every** (Standard level) **36 through** (Advanced level) **37 possum** (Intermediate level) **38 goat** (Intermediate level) **39 goose** (Intermediate level) **40 baking** (Standard level) **41 tasted** (Intermediate level) **42 grandparents** (Intermediate level) **43 impossible** (Advanced level) **44 lawn** (Advanced level) **45 stale** (Advanced level) **46 lioness** (Intermediate level) **47 female** (Advanced level) **48 rooster** (Intermediate level) **49 fox** (Intermediate level) **50 foal** (Advanced level)

1 The correct pronoun to refer to *my mum* is *she*. *They* is plural. *You* is second person.

2 The connective *so* links the two clauses. The other connecting words don't make sense in the sentence.

3 People sit *at* a table.

4 *Swooped* is the action verb in the sentence. *Swooped* is what the owl did.

5 The word *hot* describes the day.

6 *An* is the correct word to use before a noun that starts with a vowel sound (***a e i o u***).

7 These are instructions. They are written to address the reader so 'your' is appropriate.

8 The verb *be* is needed.

9 The preposition *of* starts the phrase.

10 The word *and* adds information.

11 The verb *bought* is incorrect in this sentence. It is the wrong tense (past). The correct action verb is *buy*. *Mum said they could also <u>buy</u> ice-creams.*

12 *Go to school* is a sentence that is a command. It starts with an action verb, *Go*. A sentence must include at least one verb.

13 *Slowly* is an adverb. Adverbs add information about the verb, by telling **how**. The verb is *chomped*. Ask: how did the silkworm chomp? The answer is *slowly*.

14 This sentence is a statement. It should start with a capital letter and end in a full stop. The word *library* is a common noun and does not need a capital letter. Common nouns name everyday things.

15 *Have you finished your work?* is the only question and so is the only option which should end in a question mark.

16 A comma belongs between items in a list of three or more things but not before *and*. The sentence is a statement and so should end with a full stop.

17 The correct connecting word is *because*. *Because* links the two ideas through reason.

18 The noun is *watermelon*. Nouns name people, places, animals and things.

19 *Glendale Primary School* is the proper noun name of the school and so needs capital letters. The sentence should start with a capital letter and end in a full stop.

20 Speech marks go around what is being said in the sentence, including the comma: "I saw a flying saucer," said Louie.

21 Conjunctions such as *and*, *but*, *so* and *because* join clauses so that they make sense.

22 The pronouns can refer to the nouns. Pronouns can be singular (I, he, she, it) or plural (we, they).

23 The sentence is a question. It begins with a capital letter and a question word *What*. It ends with a question mark.

24 The adverbs tell more about the verbs *ran*, *laughed*, *ate*, *listened*.

25 In the second sentence *It* is used to refer to the noun group *The hungry tiger* from the first sentence.

26 *Rare* rhymes with *stare, pare, hare* and *fare*. It is spelt with 'are'. The same sound is spelt

differently in *chair, bear, heir, they're, there* and *their*.

27 *Tripped* is a past-tense verb, formed by adding the suffix 'ed' to *trip*. Note the double ***p***.

28 *Scissors* is a plural noun. There is no singular for *scissors*. You can have *one pair of scissors* or *ten pairs of scissors*.

29 *Sunburnt* is a compound word, made of *sun* + *burnt*. Note the 'ur' which is also used in *churn* and *return*.

30 *Scratching* is the verb *scratch* with the suffix 'ing'. Note the 'tch' which can also be found in *catch, etch, hatch, pitch, ditch, watch, witch* and *stitch*.

31 *Quickly* contains the suffix 'ly'. *Quickly* is an adverb. It tells **how**. Note the 'qu' which says 'kw'.

32 *Watch* uses ***a*** to say the short ***o*** sound as in *what, was* and *squad*. Note the 'tch'.

33 *Sorry* has double 'rr'. The ***y*** ending is also used in *funny, silly* and *happy*.

34 *Learn* uses 'ear' to spell the sound also found in *churn, fern* and *first*.

35 *Every* is a basic sight word. Learn to spell it automatically.

36 The 'ough' letter combination is not common and should be learned automatically. It has the long 'oo' sound.

37 *Possum* ends in 'um', not 'em'.

38 *Goat* has the 'oa' spelling for a long ***o*** sound that is also found in *boat, gloat, float* and *groan*. The same sound is spelt differently in *toe, folk, dough* and *home*.

39 *Goose* is spelt with 'oo' which has the same sound as in *boot, spoon* and *soon*.

40 *Baking* is made by adding the suffix 'ing' to the word *bake*. When adding the suffix 'ing' to words that end in ***e*** you usually drop the ***e***: *drive* → *driving, hope* → *hoping, rake* → *raking, write* → *writing*.

41 *Tasted* is made up of the word *taste* and the suffix 'ed'. You need to drop the final ***e*** before adding the suffix 'ed'.

42 *Grandparents* is a compound word. Remember the two individual words *grand* and *parents* so that you remember to keep the ***d***.

43 *Impossible* has the prefix 'im' to make an opposite meaning: *possible* → *impossible*. It also has the suffix 'ible'. Some words use the suffix 'able', e.g. *delectable*.

44 *Lawn* is spelt with 'aw', also found in *paw, raw, prawn* and *crawl*.

45 *Stale* has a long ***a*** vowel sound because of the final ***e***. This ***a–e*** combination is also found in *name, change, pale* and *gale*. The same sound but with different spellings is found in *pail, day, break, rein, weight* and *they*.

46 A *lioness* is a female lion.

47 *Female* has the word *male* at the end.

48 *Rooster* has an 'oo' spelling pattern that makes the same sound in *room, broom, choose, loose*.

49 The 'ox' in *fox* sounds like it should be spelt 'ks'.

50 The two letters 'oa' in *foal* make a single sound. Other words with this spelling pattern include *goal* and *loan*. The letters 'oa' make different sounds in other words; e.g. *foam, boat, goanna*.

Standard level

READING SAMPLE Test 1

Go to the **inside back cover** for a guide to question types.

Email

Page 63

1 B (Intermediate level) **2 A** (Standard level)
3 C, D (Standard level) **4 B** (Standard level)
5 A (Standard level) **6 C** (Standard level)

1 This is a **synthesis type of question**. To work out the answer you have to read the whole text. You read that Jordie says *Grandparents are funny* (see line 12). You also read *Nonno likes to cook. His* … (see line 7). *Nonno* is a grandfather and so *Nonna* is a grandmother.

2 This is an **inferring type of question**. To work out the answer you have to 'read between the lines'. You read *Nonno and I take Jack for a walk to the beach … He … fetches sticks* (see lines 4–5).

3 This is a **language type of question**. To work out the answer you have to read the text carefully, especially the section that is quoted: *Spaghetti alla Pescatore* [is] *spaghetti with seafood* (see lines 7–8). Seagulls and sticks are not seafood or spaghetti.

4 This is a **fact-finding type of question**. The answer is a fact in the text. You read *Nonna is* *busy every day at the shop with Aunty Maria* (see line 10).

5 This is an **inferring type of question**. To work out the answer you have to 'read between the lines'. You read that Nonna (Jordie's grandmother) *is busy every day at the shop* (see line 10). Nonno has time to walk the dog and cook with Jordie so it can be inferred that Nonno does not work in the shop with Aunty Maria.

6 This is a **judgement type of question**. You read *I am having a great time* (see line 4). Jordie then continues his email to his parents by describing all the things he is doing with Nonno. You can work out that Jordie is having a great time doing things with Nonno so Nonno must be fun. The text states that Nonno walks to the beach every day so he is not lazy. Nonno has interests such as cooking so he is not boring. There is no evidence in the text to say that Nonno is cranky. The most appropriate answer is 'fun'.

Celebrating with food

Page 64

7 C (Standard level) **8 B** (Standard level) **9 C** (Standard level)
10 A (Standard level) **11 B, D** (Standard level)
12 B (Advanced level)

7 This is a **fact-finding type of question**. The answer is a fact in the text. You read *ANZAC biscuits are made with oats* (see lines 7–8).

8 This is a **fact-finding type of question**. The answer is a fact in the text. You read *Oranges and tangerines are important fruit at Chinese New Year* (see line 9).

9 This is a **fact-finding type of question**. The answer is a fact in the text. You read '*kook soo sang*' means '*noodle banquet*' (see line 12).

10 This is a **fact-finding type of question**. The answer is a fact in the text. You read that piñatas are *made to hold small items such as sweets* (see line 14).

11 This is a **fact-finding type of question**. The answer is a fact in the text. You read *Long noodles represent a long marriage and a long life* (see lines 12–13).

12 This is a **synthesis type of question**. To work out the answer you have to read the final paragraph to work out that the statement 'It's important to hurt people with tomatoes' is not true.

School fete brainstorming chart

Page 65

13 B (Advanced level) **14 A** (Standard level)
15 B (Standard level) **16 C** (Standard level)
17 D (Intermediate level) **18 B** (Standard level)

13 This is a **judgement type of question**. Look at the layout of the text and the ideas written to work out that *brainstorming* means 'creating a list of ideas'.

14 This is a **fact-finding type of question**. The answer is a fact in the text. You read *face painting—Year 6 students can be in charge* (see lines 21–22).

15 This is a **fact-finding type of question**. The answer is a fact in the text. You read *pancakes with fruit and yoghurt* (see line 7).

16 This is a **fact-finding type of question**. The answer is a fact in the text. You read *invite a local dance group to perform, e.g. 'Dancing All Stars'* (see lines 29–30).

17 This is a **fact-finding type of question**. The answer is a fact in the text. You read *car boot sale—each car owner can pay the school a fee* (see lines 32–33).

18 This is a **fact-finding type of question**. The answer is a fact in the text. You read *raffle—what prizes? ask local businesses to donate prizes* (see lines 11–14).

Long-distance dad

Page 66

19 C (Standard level) **20 D** (Standard level)
21 B (Standard level) **22 A** (Intermediate level)
23 D (Intermediate level) **24 D** (Advanced level)

19 This is a **synthesis type of question**. To work out the answer you have to read the whole text. You read that Ben *thought about what his mother had said. His parents were getting a divorce* (see lines 3–4). Ben goes on to think about the impact this would have on his life such as his father moving a long way away.

20 This is a **fact-finding type of question**. The answer is a fact in the text. You read *His dad had moved out of the house three months ago* (see line 4).

Year 2 Literacy Sample Online-style Test Answers

21 This is a **fact-finding type of question**. The answer is a fact in the text. You read *He and his dad liked to try out new recipes together* (see lines 13–14).

22 This is a **fact-finding type of question**. The answer is a fact in the text. You read *Now his dad was moving a long way away. Ben didn't like it, not one little bit* (see line 15).

23 This is a **fact-finding type of question**. The answer is a fact in the text. You read *His dad was going to live on the other side of the country. He had a new job* (see lines 6–7).

24 This is a **judgement type of question**. The text deals with the issue of the parents' divorce and the fact that the father is now moving across the country. The distance of the separation is the biggest problem for Ben who was dealing well with his father living separately until his mother told him about the divorce and the fact that his father was moving a long way away.

The Tasmanian devil

Page 67

25 C (Standard level) **26 A** (Standard level)
27 A, D (Standard level) **28 A** (Standard level)
29 C (Standard level) **30 B** (Intermediate level)
31 see below (Standard level)

25 This is a **fact-finding type of question**. The answer is a fact in the text. You read *Tasmanian devils live in Tasmania* (see line 2).

26 This is a **fact-finding type of question**. The answer is a fact in the text. You read *Marsupials are animals that have pouches for their babies* (see lines 3–4).

27 This is a **fact-finding type of question**. The answers are facts in the text (see lines 7–9).

28 This is a **fact-finding type of question**. The answer is a fact in the text. You read *They have wide, strong jaws for eating bones and fur* (see line 9).

29 This is a **fact-finding type of question**. The answer is a fact in the text. You read *This disease has killed a large number of devils … Devils are also killed by cars, dogs and foxes* (see lines 15–16).

30 This is a **synthesis type of question**. Read the whole text to understand that the text is a report. It gives lots of facts about Tasmanian devils. Its purpose is to inform.

31 This is a **fact-finding type of question**. These noun groups can be found in the text: strong jaws; black fur; scary screeching; white patches. This answer can be worked out from the text: pouched animal (see lines 3–4).

Down came the spider

Page 68

32 B (Standard level) **33 D** (Advanced level)
34 A (Intermediate level) **35 A** (Intermediate level)
36 C (Intermediate level) **37 Answers will vary.** (Standard level) **38 B** (Intermediate level) **39 see below** (Standard level)

32 This is a **fact-finding type of question**. The answer is a fact in the text. You read that the book is *by much-loved author Fu Yeng* (see line 1).

33 This is a **synthesis type of question**. You read of its *fantastic adventures* (see line 15) and that it is *Available now in all good bookstores* (see line 17). Read the whole text to recognise that it is a persuasive text written to convince readers to buy the book.

34 This is a **judgement type of question**. The text describes Diana's adventures. Readers can judge that the book is full of action.

35 This is a **judgement type of question**. Read the whole text and you can judge that Diana is adventurous rather than shy. You read of her *fantastic adventures* (see line 15). She might be funny but this is not evident in the text. She is possibly always hungry but this cannot be assumed through reading the text.

36 This is a **fact-finding type of question**. The answer is a fact in the text. You read *This time, our heroine DIANA travels with her parents into the deepest darkest jungles of Africa* (see lines 2–6).

37 This is a **judgement type of question**. This question asks for your opinion. You could say you would like to read a book like *Down came the spider* or that you would not like to read it, but you must say why. You could say that the book sounds exciting and interesting. You could say that you like African animals. You could say that you don't like adventure stories. Your opinion can't be wrong but you must give a reason for it.

38 This is a **language type of question**. To work out the answer you have to read the text carefully. The *latest* adventure means the most recent book in the series.

39 This is a **language type of question**. To work out the answer you have to read the text carefully. The action verbs are *travels*, *tangles*, *tumbles* and *treks*. Note that these verbs are examples of alliteration. They all begin with *t*.

Intermediate level

READING SAMPLE Test 2

How to prevent tooth decay

Page 69

1 D (Intermediate level) **2 A** (Intermediate level)
3 C (Intermediate level) **4 B** (Standard level)
5 D (Advanced level) **6 C** (Intermediate level)

1 This is a **fact-finding type of question**. The answer is a fact in the text. You read *Teeth have a hard outer layer of tooth enamel. This enamel helps to protect teeth* (see lines 2–3).

2 This is a **fact-finding type of question**. The answer is a fact in the text. You read *Using fluoride toothpaste helps strengthen tooth enamel* (see line 14).

3 This is a **fact-finding type of question**. The answer is a fact in the text. You read *Bacteria eat the sugars and make acid* (see line 8).

4 This is a **fact-finding type of question**. The answer is a fact in the text. You read *The acid destroys tooth enamel* (see line 8).

5 This is a **synthesis type of question**. You need to read the whole text to understand that A, B and C are true but D is not true.

6 This is a **fact-finding type of question**. The answer is a fact in the text. You read *Brushing your teeth twice a day helps to remove the plaque* (see line 10).

A frog's lament

Page 70

7 B (Standard level) **8 C** (Standard level) **9 D** (Intermediate level) **10 A** (Advanced level) **11 B** (Intermediate level)
12 Answers will vary. (Advanced level)

7 This is a **fact-finding type of question**. The answer is a fact in the text. You read *One day a tiny little frog, only two and a half centimetres long* (see line 2).

8 This is a **fact-finding type of question**. The answer is a fact in the text. You read that the frog is searching for *other Corroboree frogs* (see line 5).

9 This is a **language type of question**. To work out the answer you have to read the text carefully. You read *The tadpole sobbed* (see line 9). *Sobbed* is another word for 'cried'. If the frog was sobbing or crying it was upset.

10 This is a **fact-finding type of question**. The answer is a fact in the text. You read *The water pools are drying out too quickly. The tadpoles don't have time to turn into frogs. They're dying too* (see lines 15–16).

11 This is a **fact-finding type of question**. The answer is a fact in the text. You read *The fungus killed the frogs* (see lines 11–12).

12 This is a **synthesis type of question**. Your answer should make sense in the context of the story. You might suggest that the frogs ask scientists for help to defeat the fungus or for people to do something about climate change. Or you might suggest the frogs ask other animals to help carry water to the tadpole's pool.

Our favourite-fruit graph

Page 71

13 B (Standard level) **14 B** (Standard level)
15 D (Standard level) **16 C** (Intermediate level)
17 B (Intermediate level) **18 A** (Intermediate level)

13 This is a **fact-finding type of question**. The answer is shown in the graph. Two students prefer oranges.

14 This is a **fact-finding type of question**. The answer is shown in the graph. Bananas are the most popular fruit.

15 This is a **fact-finding type of question**. The answer is shown in the graph. Pears are the least popular fruit.

16 This is a **fact-finding type of question**. The answer is a fact in the text. You read *most said that they love fresh fruit as well as dried and tinned fruit* (see line 8).

17 This is a **fact-finding type of question**. The answer is a fact in the text. You read *bananas went soggy too easily when packed in lunchboxes* (see lines 4–5).

18 This is a **fact-finding type of question**. The answer is a fact in the text. You read *Students in our class voted for their favourite fruit. The top eight fruits are shown on the graph* (see lines 2–3).

Pelican

Page 72

19 C (Advanced level) **20 B** (Intermediate level)
21 B (Intermediate level) **22 C** (Intermediate level)
23 B (Intermediate level) **24 D** (Advanced level)
25 see below (Advanced level)

19 This is a **language type of question**. To work out the answer you have to read the text carefully, especially the section that is quoted. The poet uses *magnificent (see line 4)* and *amazing (see line 31)* to describe pelicans. These words tell readers that the poet is impressed by pelicans.

20 This is a **fact-finding type of question**. The answer is a fact in the text. You read The poem says: *Looking for food / it plunges its bill / under the surface. / Scooping the fish / into its pouch / then / gulping them / down (see lines 16–23).*

21 This is a **fact-finding type of question**. The answer is a fact in the text. You read that the pelican *paddles / on water. / Looking for food (see lines 14–16)* and then *plunges its bill / under the surface (see lines 17–18).*

22 This is a **language type of question**. To work out the answer you have to read the text carefully. You read *Looking for food … gulping them / down (see lines 16 and 22)*. The poem uses *gulping* for 'swallowing'.

23 This is a **language type of question**. To work out the answer you have to read the text carefully. You read *On giant wings / it glides / through the air (see lines 10–12).* The poem uses *glides* to tell how the pelican moves through the air.

24 This is a **judgement type of question**. You read *The pelican / magnificent bird (see lines 2–4).* The main message or idea in the poem is that pelicans are 'terrific birds'.

25 This is a **fact-finding type of question**. The noun groups (descriptive adjective and noun) are used in the text: *magnificent bird (line 4)*; *Long neck (line 9)*; *lofty height (line 30)*; *Belly now full (line 25)*; *giant feet (line 13).*

A trip to the museum

Page 73

26 B (Standard level) **27 C** (Advanced level)
28 B (Intermediate level) **29 A** (Intermediate level)
30 D (Advanced level) **31 A** (Intermediate level)
32 C (Intermediate level)

26 This is a **fact-finding type of question**. The answer is a fact in the text. You read that the children *caught our bus back to school (see lines 16–17).*

27 This is an **inferring type of question**. To work out the answer you have to 'read between the lines'. You can work out the answer based on what the text says the curator does: *He told us all about the paintings we were going to see (see lines 5–6).*

28 This is a **synthesis type of question**. To work out the answer you have to read the whole text. It begins with *Yesterday, all the children in my class went on an excursion to the museum (see lines 2–3).* It then describes the trip and finishes with *We arrived back at school just in time for assembly (see line 17).* From this you can work out that the purpose of the text is to tell readers about an event that has happened, the class excursion to the museum.

29 This is an **inferring type of question**. To work out the answer you have to 'read between the lines'. You can work out that the writer is a class member. Pronouns *we* and *us* are used. The text says: *all the children in my class (see line 2).*

30 This is a **fact-finding type of question**. The answer is a fact in the text. You read *Warakurna is in the middle of Australia, about 330 kilometres west of Uluru (see lines 7–8).*

31 This is a **fact-finding type of question**. The answer is a fact in the text. You read *We ate lunch outside the museum entrance (see line 16).*

32 This is a **judgement type of question**. The writer states that it was *interesting* to learn about the lives of the Warakurna People *(line 14)*. This is the only opinion given so you cannot judge any of the other answers correct.

Our adventure playground

Page 74

33 B (Intermediate level) **34 C** (Standard level)
35 B (Advanced level) **36 D** (Standard level)
37 A (Intermediate level) **38 D** (Advanced level)
39 C, D (Advanced level)

33 This is a **judgement type of question**. You read *There is a playground in town that I love. It is the best playground I have ever seen (see lines 2–4).* The writer recommends the playground. You can judge that the writer is excited about the playground.

34 This is a **fact-finding type of question**. The answer is a fact in the text. You read that the water play area is *mainly for toddlers* (see line 11). The frog fountains are in the water play area. *Little children have a great time splashing under the frogs* (see line 12).

35 This is a **synthesis type of question**. To work out the answer you have to read the whole text. You read *It is the best playground I have ever seen* (see lines 3–4). You also read *I recommend our adventure playground* (see lines 16–17). From this you can work out that the purpose of the text is to tell readers how good the playground is.

36 This is a **fact-finding type of question**. The answer is a fact in the text. You read *The older children like the bike track* (see line 10).

37 This is a **language type of question**. To work out the answer you have to read the text carefully. You read *Entry is free* (see line 17). *Entry* means 'to go in', so to go into the park costs nothing.

38 This is a **judgement type of question**. You read that the bike track is popular with older children, that little children enjoy the water play area and that families can have barbecues and use the shaded picnic tables or buy food. You also read *I recommend our adventure playground to all families with children of any age* (see lines 16–17). Readers can make a judgement that the park is suitable for families with children of all ages.

39 This is a **judgement type of question**. The writer of *Our adventure playground* shares an opinion about the playground and recommends that people use it. This is persuasion. The writer of *A trip to a museum* recounts events. It is an informative text. There is no attempt to persuade people to go on the excursion.

Advanced level

READING SAMPLE Test 3

Recycling glass

Page 75

1 D (Standard level) **2 [4, 2, 3, 1]** (Advanced level)
3 A (Standard level) **4 D** (Intermediate level)
5 C (Advanced level) **6 B** (Advanced level)

1 This is a **fact-finding type of question**. The answer is a fact in the text. You read *Recycling means reusing things* (see line 2).

2 This is a **synthesis type of question**. To work out the answer you have to read the whole text and in particular items 3, 4, 5 and 6 to sort out the sequence of events.

3 This is a **fact-finding type of question**. The answer is a fact in the text. You read *crushed glass is called cullet* (see line 12).

4 This is a **fact-finding type of question**. The answer is a fact in the text. You read *the colouring agent in glass cannot be removed so brown glass will always be recycled as brown glass, and green as green glass* (see lines 7–9).

5 This is a **synthesis type of question**. You need to read paragraph one and the final paragraph to work out that it is not true that recycling is difficult. You read *Glass can be reused over and over and over again* (see lines 2–3) and *It is quick and easy to recycle glass* (see line 15).

6 This is an **inferring type of question**. To work out the answer you have to 'read between the lines'. You read *It is quick and easy to recycle glass and cheaper than making new glass. Recycling glass saves lots of carbon dioxide from going into the air. Carbon dioxide is a greenhouse gas. Greenhouse gases are unhealthy for planet Earth* (see lines 15–17). You can infer that the writer's opinion about recycling is that it is good for planet Earth.

Clever birds

Page 76

7 C (Intermediate level) **8 B** (Advanced level)
9 D (Intermediate level) **10 B** (Advanced level)
11 B (Advanced level) **12 D** (Advanced level)

7 This is a **fact-finding type of question**. The answer is a fact in the text. You read *Crows, rooks and ravens make up the 'corvid' family of birds* (see lines 2–3).

8 This is a **synthesis type of question**. To work out the answer you have to read the whole text. The whole text is about corvids being *clever birds* (see line 1).

9 This is a **fact-finding type of question**. The answer is a fact in the text. You read *Corvids use tools such as sticks to get food from cracks in rocks* (see lines 5–6).

10 This is a **synthesis type of question**. There is information in the text that supports with each statement except that 'All farmers hate corvids'. The text says that *Some farmers say that corvids kill their lambs* (see line 18). This does not mean that all farmers hate corvids.

11 This is a **fact-finding type of question**. The answer is a fact in the text. You read *Some crows in Japan have shown they understand how traffic lights work. They place nuts on the road to be run over by cars. Then they wait for the traffic lights to turn red so the cars stop. Then the birds collect their crushed nuts while it's safe* (see lines 8–11).

12 This is a **fact-finding type of question**. Read paragraph two carefully and read each possible answer carefully. The direct result of the crow dropping stones was that *the water level rose* (see line 13).

Dear Zoo

Page 77

13 B (Advanced level) **14 A** (Advanced level)
15 B, E (Advanced level) **16 C** (Standard level)
17 A (Standard level) **18 D** (Advanced level)

13 This is a **synthesis type of question**. To work out the answer you have to read the whole text to understand that Amira's purpose in writing the letter was to give her opinion about the zoo, such as *The chimps at Taronga have a wonderful place to play* (see line 15).

14 This is a **fact-finding type of question**. The answer is a fact in the text. You read *the wonderful chimpanzee home* (see line 10).

15 This is a **fact-finding type of question**. The answers are facts in the text. You read *I hope can be a zoo keeper and work at Taronga Zoo* (see lines 16-17).

16 This is a **fact-finding type of question**. The answer is a fact in the text. You read *She loves Taronga Zoo too* (see line 18).

17 This is a **fact-finding type of question**. The answer is a fact in the text. You read *Mum says that she will buy me a Zoo Friends Membership for my birthday* (see lines 17–18).

18 This is a **judgement type of question**. You read *I want to thank you for looking after all your animals so well* (see line 13). You can work out that Amira is happy about Taronga Zoo and that it is a good place to visit, so readers will feel good about Taronga Zoo.

Jackie and the magic seeds

Page 78

19 D (Standard level) **20 B** (Intermediate level)
21 A (Standard level) **22 B** (Advanced level)
23 B (Intermediate level) **24 C** (Advanced level)

19 This is a **fact-finding type of question**. The answer is a fact in the text. You read *Jackie could not afford to buy even one* [tomato]. *She left the shop* (see lines 5–6).

20 This is a **fact-finding type of question**. The answer is a fact in the text. You read *When she showed the seeds to her father he was very angry. He said that Jackie had been tricked* (see lines 12–13).

21 This is a **fact-finding type of question**. The answer is a fact in the text. You read *He threw the seeds out the window* (see lines 14–15).

22 This is a **language type of question**. To work out the answer you have to read the text carefully, especially the section that is quoted: *To her astonishment she discovered that the seeds had already started to grow* (see lines 16–17). You can work out the meaning of astonishment by examining the way it is used and your understanding of the meaning of the text. Jackie would have been surprised to see that the plants had grown so quickly. *To her astonishment* could be replaced with 'To her surprise' and mean the same thing.

23 This is a **judgement type of question**. The text is a narrative—it tells the story of Jackie and the magic seeds. Its purpose is to entertain.

24 This is an **inferring type of question**. To work out the answer you have to 'read between the lines'. The clue to what will happen next in the story is in the last two sentences: *Jackie wondered what was at the top of the stalks. She looked for a foothold* (see lines 19–20). Jackie is curious about what is at the top of the stalks and because she looks for a foothold readers can tell she is going to climb up.

Year 2 Literacy Sample Online-style Test Answers

Note to Fred

Page 79

25 D (Intermediate level) **26 A** (Intermediate level)
27 B (Standard level) **28 A** (Intermediate level)
29 C (Intermediate level) **30 C** (Standard level)
31 see below (Intermediate)

25 This is a **fact-finding type of question**. The answer is a fact in the text. You read that the letter is signed *Your friend, Red* (see lines 16–17).

26 This is a **fact-finding type of question**. The answer is a fact in the text. You read *Please will you go and check on my grandma and take her the cookies?* (see lines 8–10).

27 This is a **fact-finding type of question**. The answer is a fact in the text. You read that Red says to *watch out for wolves* (see line 14).

28 This is a **fact-finding type of question**. The answer is a fact in the text. You read the label on the map that tells Fred that Grandma's house has a red door.

29 This is a **fact-finding type of question**. The answer is a fact in the text. You read the label on the map that tells Fred that the wolf likes to hide behind the biggest tree.

30 This is a **fact-finding type of question**. The answer is a fact in the text. You read *It's an easy walk* (see line 13).

31 This is an **inferring type of question**. The noun groups (descriptive adjective and noun) can be either found in the text or inferred from the text: *sick girl*; *sneaky wolf*; *easy walk*; *biggest tree*; *good friend*.

Olympics

Page 80

32 B (Standard level) **33 A** (Advanced level)
34 B (Intermediate level) **35 A** (Intermediate level)
36 C (Advanced level) **37 D** (Advanced level)
38 C (Intermediate level) **39 C** (Advanced level)

32 This is a **fact-finding type of question**. The answer is a fact in the text. You read *The Olympic Games and the Paralympic Games are held every four years* (see lines 2–3).

33 This is a **fact-finding type of question**. The answer is a fact in the text. You read *I like the hockey because it is fast and exciting* (see line 9).

34 This is a **fact-finding type of question**. The answer is a fact in the text. You read *My sister likes the swimming relays … She also likes the running relays* (see lines 13–14).

35 This is a **fact-finding type of question**. The answer is a fact in the text. You read *My brother … competes in the long jump in our school athletics carnivals* (see lines 11–12).

36 This is a **language type of question**. To find the answer you have to read the text carefully, especially the section that is quoted: *Mum really likes it when a developing country in Africa wins a medal … Mum likes to cheer for the underdog* (see lines 16 and 18). *Underdog* is a word that is used for the player or team that is not expected to win in a competition. When the writer says that *Mum likes to cheer for the underdog* it means that *Mum* supports countries that don't win many medals and are not expected to win very often. These countries would be the *underdog*s of the Olympics.

37 This is a **synthesis type of question**. To work out the answer you have to read the whole text. The writer shares family members' opinions about the Olympics.

38 This is a **fact-finding type of question**. The answer is a fact in the text. You read *soccer, which I play* (see line 10).

39 This is a **judgement type of question**. The main idea in the text is that different people enjoy participating in different sports and they also enjoy watching different sports in events such as the Olympic and Paralympic Games.

Year 2 Literacy Sample Online-style Test Answers

WRITING Sample Tests 1, 2 and 3

Pages 81–83

Go to **pages 123–128** for, Intermediate and Advanced Writing samples for Sample Tests 1, 2 and 3.

Go to **pages 100–101** for Marking checklists for Sample Tests 1 and 2:

- Persuasive text (page 100)
- Narrative text (pages 100–101).

WRITING Sample Test 3: Description text

Page 83

Marking checklist for a description text

Read the text. Gather an overall impression first, then read the text a second time to consider each of the ten assessment criteria below. Tick each correct point.

Audience

☐ Is the text interesting/relevant for its target audience?

☐ Does the description make sense?

Text structure

☐ Does the text have an appropriate structure?

☐ Does it include an introduction to orient the reader to setting, people and time?

☐ Does the body of the text have enough detail?

☐ Does it have a concluding statement or summing up, if appropriate?

Ideas

☐ Are the ideas sequenced logically?

☐ Are the ideas thought through?

☐ Is the writer able to write knowledgeably about the subject?

Character and setting

☐ Are the writer's opinions evident in the text, as appropriate?

☐ Is the subject well described?

Vocabulary

☐ Is there sufficient detail?

☐ Are noun groups (nouns and adjectives) used effectively?

☐ Are verbs used appropriately for actions and activity?

☐ Are verbs used consistently?

☐ Are pronouns used consistently?

Cohesion

☐ Does the text flow logically?

☐ Are connectives used to link ideas (e.g. as well as, also, but, although)

☐ Is noun–pronoun reference accurate (e.g. Mum—she)?

Paragraphing

☐ Are paragraphs used to organise aspects of the topic?

☐ Are paragraphs built around topic sentences?

Sentence structure

☐ Are a variety of sentence structures evident, as appropriate (simple, compound, complex; direct and indirect speech)?

Punctuation

☐ Is sentence punctuation evident and accurate?

☐ Are there capital letters for sentence beginnings and proper nouns?

☐ Are commas and full stops used accurately and consistently?

Spelling

☐ How accurate is the spelling?

☐ What attempts have been made to spell unknown words?

☐ Are the attempts phonetically correct or readable?

☐ Does the student spell simple, common, difficult and challenging words correctly?

Writing Mini Test 1

People in cities should not be allowed to own dogs

I think that people in cities should be allowed to own dogs.

Dogs are good company **if** you are old and you live by yourself it's good to have a dog. My grandpa has a dog. Its name is Giuseppe. Giuseppe is Grandpa's best friend. They do everything together. I think my grandpa would be sad without Giuseppe. He **wood** be lonely if he didn't have his dog. He walks Giuseppe every day so they both get some **exsicise**. **my** grandpa is fit because of Giuseppe.

Dogs are good for children. **Its** good for children to have pets.

Dogs bark if they hear a **theef** so they protect people. This is important in a city because there are bad people in the city. People in cities have a right to own a dog. I think anyone who wants a dog should be **aloud** to own one. Make **shure** your dog **dosen't** bark all the time.

Structure

Audience

The text provides enough information to support an audience's understanding of the writer's position and begins to engage the reader through personal connection.

Persuasive techniques

The text contains personal opinions: *I think … should be allowed … a right …*

*dogs are good … **Its** good for children ….*

Text is emotive: *Grandpa would be lonely … they protect people … bad people*

Text structure

The structure is appropriate. There is an underdeveloped, one-sentence introduction. The body of the text presents three arguments but with limited reasons.

There is no elaboration for the argument *Dogs are good for children. **Its** good for children to have pets.*

There is a concluding statement which restates the writer's position: *I think anyone who wants a dog should be **aloud** to own one.*

The writer gives personal justification for opinions.

There is no evidence that the writer has considered problems that people in cities might have with dogs except that barking dogs annoy people.

Paragraphing

Ideas are grouped logically. The introduction is a single sentence and could have been further developed. The paragraph *Dogs are good for children* could have been further developed to give reasons why.

Cohesion

Writer uses personal pronouns *I* and *he*.

There is simple noun–pronoun reference: *dogs–they*.

Relative pronoun reference appears. This in paragraph 4 refers to the previous sentence: *Dogs bark if they hear a **theef** so they protect people. <u>This</u> is important …*

Connecting words are used to link cause and effect of ideas: *if, because* and *so*.

The final paragraph restates the writer's position on the topic, as introduced in the first paragraph.

Language and ideas

Vocabulary

Single nouns and simple adjectives are used, e.g. *old*.

Vocabulary relates to the topic but is somewhat limited, e.g. repetition of the word *good*.

Sentence structure

The text consists of mainly grammatically correct simple and compound sentences, e.g. simple sentence: *Giuseppe is Grandpa's best friend.*

There is a compound sentence with the conjunction *so*: *He walks Giuseppe every day **so** they both get some **exsicise**.*

The last sentence is a command that is out of place: *Make **shure** your dog **dosen't** bark all the time.*

Ideas

The writing contains many simple ideas. The writer relates the topic to personal knowledge but there is no evidence of sustained thinking beyond the personal.

Some ideas are simplistic: *Dogs bark if they hear a **theef** … there are bad people in the city.*

Punctuation

There is some appropriate sentence punctuation.

Contractions in *didn't* and *doesn't* are used accurately.

Contraction in *its* is inaccurate: It's good for children …

The proper noun has a capital letter: *Giuseppe.*

Spelling

There is correct spelling of simple and common words but incorrect spelling of challenging words: *exercise, thief, sure, doesn't*

Aloud and *wood* are used instead of homophones *allowed* and *would.*

Plurals are correctly used: *people.*

Please note that this sample has not been written under test conditions. However, it gives you a standard to aim for. It contains **mistakes** to give you an idea of the standard written at Intermediate level.

Writing Mini Test 1

Structure

Audience
The writer outlines the issue so that readers can easily understand what the text is going to be about. This gives a context for the arguments.

Persuasive techniques
The writer appeals to a reader's logic and values: *These dogs* [police dogs and assistance dogs] *are very important to their owners and need to be allowed …*

Text structure
The text has a clearly identifiable structure that starts with an introduction to the topic. The writer's position on the topic is clearly stated. The body of the text presents the arguments and reasons. These are sequenced logically. There is a summing-up which restates the writer's position.

Paragraphing
Ideas are grouped logically in paragraphs. Each paragraph is built around a main idea.

Cohesion
Noun–pronoun reference is used correctly: *Some people–They. Other people–They. All kinds of different dogs–They–These dogs.*
The conclusion restates the writer's position first given in the introduction.
The connective *but* is used to link through cause and effect: *I think that dogs should be allowed in cities* but *….*
A relative pronoun is used to refer to a subsequent clause (Paragraphs 1 and 4): *I think that ….*

People in cities should not be allowed to own dogs

Some people in the city own dogs. They think that dogs are terrific. Other people living in the city do not like dogs. They think dogs make too much noise and too much mess. They think dogs should be banned from cities. I think that dogs should be allowed in cities but I think that dog owners need to be more responsible for their dogs.

Dogs make great pets. They are excellent companions, especially for the elderly or people living alone. Dogs are good for children also. They teach children to be responsible for looking after things. It's good for children to learn to clean up after their dogs, too.

All kinds of different dogs live in the city and they have different jobs to do. Some are guard dogs. Some dogs work for the police. Some are guide dogs or assistance dogs. These dogs are very important to their owners and need to be allowed to live in the city.

The problem with dogs in the city is mainly noise and dog poo left on footpaths. I think that if dog owners were more responsible for their dogs then dogs would not need to be banned from cities. People who own dogs need to be more considerate of other people in the city.

Language and ideas

Vocabulary
Some precise vocabulary is used: *responsible, companions, assistance dogs, considerate, elderly.*

Sentence structure
Sentences demonstrate control over a variety of structures involving clauses.

Ideas
Each idea has an elaboration or reason. Both sides of the argument are evaluated. Ideas relate to the general community.

Punctuation
Appropriate sentence punctuation is used.
A contraction is correctly punctuated.

Spelling
Challenging words are correctly spelt.

Please note that this sample has not been written under test conditions. During a test you might not have the time to produce such a polished piece of writing. However, this sample gives you a standard to aim for.

Writing Mini Test 2

LOST

Nikki was left behind in her backyard every day when her owner went to school.

One day she jumped up and put her paws on the gate and it swung open. The gate **wosn't** locked! Nikki raced off down the street. But soon she was lost.

She heard **childrens** voices and raced towards the noise but it wosn't her owner. It was just a group of children waiting at a bus stop. She raced on.

She heard other voices and raced towards the noise but it wosn't her owner. It was just people sitting in a park. She raced on.

She heard **childrens** voices. She raced towards them and ran into the school **playgrownd**. She ran up to every child and sniffed, but it wosn't her owner.

Then she heard her **owners** voice. It called her name. She raced over to her owner and wagged her tail. She stayed at school all day and she was really happy.

Structure

Audience
The reader can follow the plot sequence easily.

Character and setting
There is some character development of the dog, *Nikki*, using verbs such as *raced* and *wagged*.
The setting is a local neighbourhood with the *bus stop*, *park* and *school* ***playgrownd***.

Text structure
There is a clearly identifiable structure: orientation, complication, series of events and resolution.

Paragraphing
Each paragraph is built around a single idea.

Cohesion
Cohesion is achieved through repetition in the story pattern: *She heard … but … She raced on.*
Simple noun–pronoun reference is used consistently: *Nikki–she.*

Language and ideas

Vocabulary
Writing is a third-person narrative with simple vocabulary.
Simple nouns are used: *paws, gate.*
Single verbs are used: *jumped, raced, heard.*
Adverb and adjective are correctly used: *really happy.*
Correct verb tense is present: *she* ***raced****; it* ***swung****;* ***called.***

Sentence structure
The writing uses mainly simple and compound sentences.

Ideas
Ideas are sustained and all relate to the central storyline however there is no depth or detail.

Punctuation
Appropriate sentence punctuation is used: *The gate* ***wosn't*** *locked!* (exclamation); ***wosn't*** *(wasn't)* (correctly punctuated contraction).
There are no possessive apostrophes in *children's, owner's.*
The proper noun correctly uses a capital letter: *Nikki.*

Spelling
Some difficult/challenging words are correctly spelt: *heard, noise, voices.*
But others are not: *playground, wasn't.*

Please note that this sample has not been written under test conditions. However, it gives you a standard to aim for. It contains **mistakes** to give you an idea of the standard written at Intermediate level.

Writing Mini Test 2

LOST

Little Nikki had been wandering the streets for hours. Now she was lost.

She had escaped from her yard when she discovered that the gate wasn't closed properly. At first she'd been excited and she just ran and ran, enjoying her freedom. Then she had followed different people who had stopped to pat her. One boy tried to pick her up but she had run away from him.

But now she was lost and hungry and getting more and more confused. She didn't recognise any of the smells around her. She didn't know what to do. It was getting dark. She didn't want to be out in the dark, all alone.

Then she heard a voice she recognised. It was calling her name. She gave a yelp. She heard the voice again. She ran towards the noise and there, on the footpath, was her owner. She was so happy. Her little tail wagged and wagged and she rolled on the ground and whimpered.

Her owner said, "Hello. I'm pleased to see you too."

Structure

Audience
The reader can follow the plot. The writer attempts to engage the reader's empathy with the character Nikki.

Character and setting
There is some character development using descriptions of Nikki's feelings and some evidence of setting related to a neighbourhood streetscape.

Text structure
There is a clearly identifiable structure. The story starts with the complication then orients the reader to character and setting. The conclusion is satisfying for the reader. The body of the story, however, is limited. There is no development of the complication or events leading to the resolution when Nikki finds her owner.

Paragraphing
Each paragraph is built around a single idea. Paragraphs are used to denote complication, orientation, events and conclusion.

Cohesion
Time connectives are used to link ideas: *now, when, then, but now, then.*

Simple noun–pronoun reference is used consistently: *Nikki–she.*

Language and ideas

Vocabulary
The writing is a third-person narrative with some precise vocabulary.

Specific choices have been made to build Nikki's character: *escaped, excited, hungry, confused, whimpered.*

Sentence structure
The writer mainly uses simple and compound sentences.

Direct speech is used in the final sentence for the resolution.

Short sentences increase the pace and build excitement at the climax.

Ideas
Ideas are sustained and all relate to the central storyline about a lost dog.

Punctuation
Appropriate sentence punctuation is used.

Direct speech is punctuated correctly.

The proper noun is correctly capitalised: *Nikki.*

Spelling
Difficult/challenging words are correctly spelt: *escaped, discovered, followed, whimpered.*

Please note that this sample has not been written under test conditions. During a test you might not have the time to produce such a polished piece of writing. However, this sample gives you a standard to aim for.

Writing Mini Test 3

Intermediate level — Sample of Recount Writing

Structure

Audience
The reader can easily follow and understand the sequence of events.

Character and setting
Some basic labelling of the setting is provided regarding the trees, water on the tracks, some of the animals.

Text structure
There is an orientation: *Last Sunday I went on a bike ride with my parents and my sister we like to go on long rides in the **nashonal** park.*

The body of the text consists of the series of events, recounted in chronological order. There is a concluding statement: *It was a great day.*

Paragraphing
There is evidence of paragraph breaks which identify the introduction, text body and conclusion. Not all paragraphs are identified accurately.

Cohesion
Cohesion is achieved using nouns related to the topic.

Events are sequenced in time: *Last Sunday, then, then, after lunch.*

Connecting words such as *but* are used to link ideas: *Last time we saw a snake but not this time.*

My cycling adventure

Last Sunday I went on a bike ride with my parents and my sister **we** like to go on long rides in the **nashonal** park. **we** put our bikes in the back of **dads** van and **dad** drove us to the park. It took a long time to get there then we went off on our bikes.

We **carryed** our backpacks with water bottles and food. We took **sandwitches** and fruit. It had been raining and the first thing we saw was all the water on the track. It was a hot day but it was cool under the trees. We saw lizards and birds. Last time we saw a snake but not this time. There were spider webs along the tracks. **we** rode for an hour and **then** we stopped to eat. **After lunch** we saw a wallaby with a joey in her pouch. **we** rode for another hour after lunch and then went back to where we'd left the van. We were all really **tiered**.

It was a great day.

Language and ideas

Vocabulary
First-person recount is sustained.

Single nouns and a few adjectives are used. The writer does not use extended noun groups to describe things in any detail.

There is correct use of past-tense verbs and pronoun reference: *we, us.*

Sentence structure
The writer mainly uses simple and compound sentences.

Ideas
Ideas are sustained and all relate to the trip.

Punctuation
There is mostly correct sentence punctuation. Some sentences do not start with capital letters.

There is a correct contraction. There is no possessive apostrophe in *dad's.*

Dad should begin with a capital letter.

Spelling
There is correct spelling of basic, common and some difficult words: *wallaby, joey, pouch.*

Challenging words are incorrectly spelt but are readable: *national, carried, tired, sandwiches.*

Please note that this sample has not been written under test conditions. However, it gives you a standard to aim for. It contains **mistakes** to give you an idea of the standard written at Intermediate level.

Writing Mini Test 3

Advanced level — Sample of Recount Writing

Structure

Audience
The reader can easily follow and understand the sequence of events.

Character and setting
Details build information: *goannas and blue-tongue lizards warming themselves on rocks in sunny clearings.*

Text structure
There is a clearly identifiable structure: title, orientation, events recounted in chronological order and resolution with personal comment: *I can't wait till our next cycling adventure.*

Paragraphing
Each paragraph is built around a single idea. The first paragraph provides the orientation and sets the scene. The body of the text is the middle three paragraphs. They tell about all the things seen during the ride. The final paragraph is the conclusion.

Cohesion
Cohesion is achieved through nouns related to the topic.
Events are sequenced in time: *Last Sunday, 9 am, by the time, but once, By the end.*
Connecting words (but) link ideas: *Last time … we saw a snake* ***but*** *not this time.*
Reference chains are correctly used: *a mother wallaby–The mother–She.*

My cycling adventure

Last Sunday I went on a bike ride with my parents and my sister. First we had to drive to the national park with our pushbikes in the back of Dad's van.

It was 9 am by the time we set off on our ride. It was starting to get quite hot but once we rode into the forest, under the tree canopy, it became much cooler.

Not far along the trail we saw a mother wallaby and her joey. The joey's head and four feet were sticking out of the pouch. It was so cute. The mother looked at us but wasn't frightened. I guess she's used to people in the park. She slowly hopped away and we rode on.

The wallaby was the most exciting thing we saw during the ride. We saw goannas and blue-tongue lizards warming themselves on rocks in sunny clearings. We heard plenty of birds and saw a few magpies and magpie-larks. Dad called them peewees. Last time we rode in the national park we saw a snake but not this time. There were some beautiful St Andrew's Cross spider webs alongside the track. The webs were amazing!

By the end of our ride we were all really tired. We'd had a great day. I can't wait till our next cycling adventure.

Language and ideas

Vocabulary
The first-person recount uses accurate vocabulary: *tree canopy, magpie-larks, blue- tongue lizards.*
Past-tense verbs are correctly used.
Noun groups with adjectives help the reader build a mental picture: *beautiful St Andrew's Cross spider webs.*
Pronoun reference is correct: *we, I.*

Sentence structure
The writer uses a variety of sentence beginnings. There are simple, compound and complex sentences.

Ideas
Ideas are sustained and all relate to the trip.

Punctuation
Appropriate sentence punctuation is used, including an exclamation.
There are correct contractions and correct possessive apostrophes.
The proper nouns are correctly capitalised: *St Andrew's Cross, Dad.*

Spelling
Difficult/challenging words are correctly spelt: *beautiful, tongue, cycling.*

Please note that this sample has not been written under test conditions. During a test you might not have the time to produce such a polished piece of writing. However, this sample gives you a standard to aim for.

Writing Sample Test 1

All schools should have a swimming pool

I agree that all schools should have a swimming pool. Swimming pools are good for children and teachers.

Firstly swimming is good **exsercise. Exsercise** is important. Swimming can keep children fit and active. If the pool is heated, you can swim all year.

The second thing is swimming can cool you down when **its** hot. **Its** hard to **consentrate** when **its** really hot. Students can have a swim to cool off so they can **consentrate** better in class. Teachers can have a swim too so they are happier.

Third it is important for everyone to know how to swim. Children drown because they can't swim. Having a swimming pool at school means that you will learn how to swim and save your own life.

I think it would be a great idea if all schools could have a swimming pool it would be fun and good **execise.**

Structure

Audience

Readers can easily follow and understand the line of argument.

Persuasive techniques

Thinking verbs are used to give personal opinions: *I agree, I think.*

There is high modality: *it is important, all schools should.*

Text structure

There is a clearly identifiable structure: an introduction which states the writer's position on the topic, then arguments and reasons listed in order of importance, and a conclusion or summing up.

Paragraphing

Each paragraph is built around a single idea with supporting detail.

Cohesion

Cohesion is achieved through *Firstly, The second thing, Third.*

Nouns relate to the topic.

There is inconsistency in labels: *students–children–you.*

Language and ideas

Vocabulary

Adverbs and adjectives are used, as well as some single precise words: *exercise, concentrate.*

Sentence structure

The writer uses compound sentences: *Children drown because …*

Some complexity is evident in sentence and clause structures: *Having a swimming pool at school means that you will learn how to swim and save your own life.*

Ideas

Several ideas are outlined and they all support the writer's position.

Punctuation

There is mostly appropriate sentence punctuation although there is a missing comma: *Firstly, swimming.*

Contractions are sometimes correct (can't) but not always: 'its' instead of *it's* for *it is.*

Spelling

Difficult words are spelt correctly.

Challenging words are spelt incorrectly: *concentrate, exercise.*

Please note that this sample has not been written under test conditions. However, it gives you a standard to aim for. It contains **mistakes** to give you an idea of the standard written at Intermediate level.

Writing Sample Test 1

All schools should have a swimming pool

I disagree with the statement that all schools should have a swimming pool. I know that many children would say that schools should have swimming pools because that would be fun but I think that swimming pools in schools are expensive and a waste of time.

It is not very practical to have a swimming pool in a school. Each class would only use the pool once or twice a week and only through summer months unless the pool is heated and that would cost too much. Cleaning the pool and regular maintenance is also costly. The money spent on a swimming pool would be better spent on putting air conditioning in every classroom.

Safety is another important reason not to have a swimming pool at school. Children can get skin cancers from spending too much time in the sun. As well, pools could be dangerous if there's only one teacher and a whole class of students. Some lower primary children are not very good swimmers so how can one teacher supervise everyone's safety?

I definitely believe that swimming pools are unnecessary in schools. Spend the money on making sure children learn to read and write. Let families teach children how to swim.

Structure

Audience
The writer's position is clear. The writer makes some attempt to let readers know the other side of the argument has been considered: *I know that many children would say that schools should have swimming pools because that would be fun but …*

Persuasive techniques
Personal opinions are given: *I disagree, I definitely believe.*
The text addresses the reader: *… how can one teacher supervise everyone's safety?*
High modality: *I know that, … swimming pools in schools are expensive and a waste of time.*
Two commands are used in the conclusion.

Text structure
There is a clearly identifiable structure: an introduction which states the writer's position on the topic; the body is developed with arguments and reasons; the conclusion is expressed strongly.

Paragraphing
Paragraph breaks are appropriate.
Each paragraph is built around a single idea with supporting detail.

Cohesion
Connecting words link ideas: *Some lower primary children are not very good swimmers so how can one teacher supervise everyone's safety?*

Language and ideas

Vocabulary
Some single precise words are used: *regular, maintenance.*
Emotive words are used: *waste, dangerous.*

Sentence structure
Some complex sentence structures appear with dependent clauses and relative pronouns: *I know that many children would say that schools should have swimming pools because that would be fun but I think that swimming pools in schools are expensive and a waste of time.*

Ideas
Several ideas are elaborated to support the writer's position.

Punctuation
The writer uses appropriate sentence punctuation.

Spelling
Challenging words are spelt correctly.

Please note that this sample has not been written under test conditions. During a test you might not have the time to produce such a polished piece of writing. However, this sample gives you a standard to aim for.

Writing Sample Test 2

Structure

Audience
The reader can easily follow and understand the story.

Character and setting
Characters are not developed. Readers are not told why the cupboard door opens to the rabbit world, why the rabbit wants the narrator to play with it, or how the narrator feels about the events.

The setting is described briefly and in simple terms.

Text structure
There is a clear text structure: an orientation to set the scene; the complication is finding another world inside the cupboard; the resolution is when the narrator returns from the fantasy world, gets back into bed and goes to sleep.

Paragraphing
There is no attempt to separate paragraphs.

Cohesion
The narrative is told in a straightforward chronological sequence.

First-person narrative is sustained. The text flows logically.

There is accurate use of referencing words: *the rabbit–she*.

Into another world

I was asleep in bed when I heard a noise **it** was coming from inside my cupboard. I **thort** my cat must **of** gone inside it to sleep. I opened the cupboard door. Inside it was daytime. Rabbits were jumping around on a **feild** eating the grass. A rabbit hopped up to me and said, "Will you play with us?" I followed the rabbit **she** took me to meet her brothers and sisters. We played a game of hide and seek. After a while I was **tierd** **I** told the rabbits goodbye. They took me back to my cupboard. I opened it and went back in my bedroom. I jumped into bed and went straight to sleep. In the morning I told Mum about my **advenchure** inside my cupboard. She said I'd just been dreaming.

Language and ideas

Vocabulary
There is limited use of descriptive language.

Single nouns are used: *rabbits, daytime.*

Incorrect grammar is used: 'must of' instead of *must have*.

Mostly single verbs are used: *heard, opened, followed.*

Sentence structure
There is mainly simple and compound sentences. All sentences are accurate grammatically.

Ideas
Ideas are relevant to the central storyline. The writer shows an understanding of fantasy genre—talking animals, other worlds accessed in magical or mysterious ways. There is limited story development, no detailed sequence of events and no climax.

Punctuation
Sentence punctuation is often correct but not always.

Direct speech is punctuated accurately.

There is a correct contraction: *I'd* (I had).

Spelling
Difficult words are sometimes correctly spelt but not always: *tired, adventure, field, thought.*

Please note that this sample has not been written under test conditions. However, it gives you a standard to aim for. It contains **mistakes** to give you an idea of the standard written at Intermediate level.

Writing Sample Test 2

Structure

Audience
The reader can easily follow and understand the story.

Character and setting
There is limited character development.
The setting is described well enough to give the story atmosphere.

Text structure
There is a clear text structure with an orientation to set the scene. The complication is finding another world inside the cupboard. There is a basic resolution when the narrator is woken from a dream.

Paragraphing
Each paragraph is built around a single idea.

Cohesion
The narrative is told in a straightforward chronological sequence.
First-person narrative is sustained. The text flows logically.
There is accurate use of referencing words: *a little white rabbit–It.*

Into another world

Knock! Knock! The noise woke me. It was the middle of the night. It was very dark. Knock! Knock! There it was again. The noise was coming from inside my cupboard. A light was shining under the door. There's no light in my cupboard, I thought. What could it be? I got out of bed and I put my ear up to the door to listen. It was quiet. I opened the door.

Inside my cupboard it was bright daylight. I saw a path leading though some green meadows. There were rabbits and flowers everywhere. Something tapped me on the foot. I looked down and there was a little white rabbit. It said, "Come on." Then it hopped away along the path. I stepped onto the footpath and my cupboard door closed behind me. I tried the handle. It was locked. I couldn't get back into my bedroom!

I ran after the rabbit. It was hopping quickly. I couldn't keep up. It ran into a forest. I followed. All of a sudden it was dark. The sun had **disappeered**. The rabbit had **disappeered**. I yelled out "Dad! Dad!"

I woke up. Dad was shaking me. "You had a bad dream," he said.

Language and ideas

Vocabulary
There is some use of descriptive language (noun groups).
The word *disappeared* is repeated rather than a synonym such as *vanished* being used to provide variety and interest.

Sentence structure
All sentences are grammatically accurate. Short sentences are used effectively to increase pace, and build suspense and drama: *I tried the handle. It was locked. I couldn't get back into my bedroom! I ran after the rabbit. It was hopping quickly. I couldn't keep up.*

Ideas
Ideas are relevant to the central storyline. The story starts well. There is a description of the fantasy world but there is limited story development. There is no series of events to build on the potential of the complication. The story ends simply.

Punctuation
There is correct sentence punctuation including a question mark, exclamation marks and speech marks, as well as a correct contraction.

Spelling
Difficult/challenging words are spelt correctly.
A **challenging** word is incorrectly spelt: *disappeared.*

Please note that this sample has not been written under test conditions. During a test you might not have the time to produce such a polished piece of writing. However, this sample gives you a standard to aim for.

Writing Sample Test 3

Structure

Audience
The text meets the needs of an audience. It includes a title to orient the reader to the topic. The subject is very familiar to the writer. The writer writes warmly and with humour. Readers can tell that the writer and Nana are close.

Character and setting
Readers can build a mental picture of Nana. The writer's point of view about the subject is apparent: *I love her too*. Readers can empathise with the writer and the relationship between great-grandmother and grandchild.

Text structure
Although the text is brief, it is well organised. It includes a title, an introduction and then ideas grouped in a logical sequence. It ends with a personal opinion.

Paragraphing
There are no paragraph breaks to separate ideas.

Cohesion
Ideas are linked logically. Use of first-person narrator is sustained: *I, me*.

References to Nana are sustained: *She … Nana … her.*

There is appropriate use of conjunctions: *Nan walks slowly but her brain is really fast.*

Accurate noun–pronoun reference is used: *Nana–she.*

My nana

I have a great-grandmother. She is 81 years old. I call her Nana. She is tiny. She has silver hair and she wears glasses. She smells like baby powder. She wears cardigans. Her **favorite** cardigan is blue with pink roses down the front. She tucks her hanky up her sleeve. Nana loves to sing old songs. She knows all the words to songs that she says she learned in school. We don't learn those songs in school any more. She thinks **thats** a shame. Nana walks slowly but her brain is really fast. She likes to play card games. My nana loves me. I love her too.

Language and ideas

Vocabulary
Basic noun groups provide some descriptive detail.

Verbs and verb groups are used appropriately.

Sentence structure
Sentences are grammatically correct.

They are mainly simple sentences: *She is 81 years old.*

There are some compound sentences: *She has silver hair and she wears glasses.*

A sentence with an adjectival phrase adds variety to the sentence types: *Her* **favorite** *cardigan is blue with pink roses down the front.*

Ideas
The writer describes Nana's physical appearance and personality characteristics.

Punctuation
Sentence punctuation is correct.

There is both a correct contraction (don't) and an incorrect one: *that's.*

Spelling
Difficult words are spelt correctly: *powder, cardigan.*

A challenging word is spelt incorrectly: *favourite.*

Please note that this sample has not been written under test conditions. However, it gives you a standard to aim for. It contains **mistakes** to give you an idea of the standard written at Intermediate level.

Writing Sample Test 3

My nana

My nana is my mother's mother's mother. She's pretty old. She just had her 81st birthday.

Nana is really skinny. She has silver hair and she wears glasses. She smells like baby powder. She always wears cardigans even when I don't think it's cold. She feels the cold. Dad says that's because she has no meat on her bones. Nana always has a hanky tucked up her sleeve.

Nana moved to a retirement village two years ago when Pop died. There is a common room where she meets up with her friends. They do yoga and other activities. On Friday nights they have Karaoke. Nana loves to sing so she enjoys that. She always sings funny old songs that she says she learned when she was a kid. I say, "Nana you were never a kid. That's a baby goat." She always laughs at my jokes. She calls me a card. I think that means I'm funny. She can also recite poems. Some of them are funny like one about a boy called Jim who was eaten by a lion. Nana makes her voice sound really posh when she recites that poem. I don't know how she remembers all those poems. Her memory is better than mine.

Nana walks slowly but her brain is really fast. She still beats me in card games, except Snap. I always beat her in Snap. You have to have quick hands to win in Snap.

My nana always says she loves me. I love her too.

Structure

Audience

The text meets the needs of an audience. It includes a title to orient the reader to the topic. The subject is very familiar to the writer. The writer writes warmly and with humour.

Character and setting

Nana is described in detail so readers can build a mental picture. The writer's point of view about the subject is apparent: *I love her too.* Readers can empathise with the writer and the relationship with a great-grandmother.

Text structure

The text is structured appropriately. It is well organised. It includes an introduction.

Ideas are grouped in a logical sequence. It ends with a personal opinion.

Paragraphing

Ideas are grouped in paragraphs according to topic.

Paragraph 1 provides introduction and background.

Paragraph 2 describes Nana's physical appearance.

Paragraph 3 describes Nana's attitude and character.

Paragraph 4 describes a different aspect of Nana's character.

Paragraph 5 is the concluding statement.

Cohesion

Ideas are linked logically. Use of first-person narrator is sustained: *I, me.*

Conjunctions are used appropriately: *Nana walks slowly but her brain is really fast.*

Noun–pronoun reference is correct: *Nana–she.*

Language and ideas

Vocabulary

Noun groups provide descriptive detail.

Verbs are used appropriately: *is, wears, always laughs, always wears, walks slowly.*

Sentence structure

A variety of sentence structures is used, including simple sentences, compound sentences and dependent clauses.

Ideas

The writer describes Nana's physical appearance, attitude and where she lives, as well as giving evidence of their relationship: *She always laughs at my jokes. She calls me a card.*

Punctuation

Correct sentence punctuation, with capital letters for sentence beginnings and proper nouns, as well as commas and full stops, is used.

Contractions are correct: *That's, don't, it's.*

Possessive apostrophes are correct: *mother's.*

Speech marks are used for quotes.

Spelling

Difficult and challenging words are spelt correctly: *retirement, karaoke, yoga.*

Please note that this sample has not been written under test conditions. During a test you might not have the time to produce such a polished piece of writing. However, this sample gives you a standard to aim for.

SPELLING WORDS FOR CONVENTIONS OF LANGUAGE TESTS

To the parent or teacher

Read the word clearly to the student. Then read the sentence with the word in it to the student. Then read the word again.

Give the student time to write an answer. If the student is not sure of the spelling tell them to make their best attempt but that it is okay to skip a word if they cannot attempt a guess.

Spelling words for Sample Test 1

Word	Example
26 garden	Worms are good for the garden.
27 started	I started reading my new book yesterday.
28 loves	Zeb loves lizards.
29 said	Dad said we could go bushwalking.
30 don't	Don't run across the road.
31 was	The storm was loud.
32 stopped	Rose stopped playing basketball this year.
33 until	Stay inside until the rain stops.
34 likes	Jenny likes hip-hop dancing.
35 are	Bananas are my favourite fruit.
36 blue	My favourite colour is blue.
37 fur	The possum had grey fur.
38 huge	Huge eyes looked out of the possum's face.
39 tail	His bushy tail rested on the branch.
40 some	Let's boil some eggs for breakfast.

Spelling words for Sample Test 2

Word	Example
26 yesterday	We had a test yesterday.
27 asked	Dad asked me to help him wash the car.
28 could	Scott wished he could get a new bike.
29 talk	"Don't talk during the test," said the teacher.
30 pieces	I eat two pieces of fruit a day.

Spelling words for Sample Test 2 continued

	Word	Example
31	lamb	A baby sheep is a lamb.
32	calf	A baby cow is a calf.
33	called	Dad called us for dinner.
34	wouldn't	I wouldn't like to be stung by a jellyfish.
35	footpath	Lily rode her bike on the footpath.
36	chain	I had to chain my bike to the fence.
37	pineapple	The pineapple was sweet.
38	grapes	I ate a bunch of red grapes.
39	tomatoes	The tomatoes were not ripe.
40	followed	I followed Mum to the car.

Spelling words for Sample Test 3

	Word	Example
26	rare	Uncle John has some rare stamps.
27	tripped	Sue tripped on the rug.
28	scissors	We had to use scissors to cut straight lines.
29	sunburnt	Don't get sunburnt.
30	scratching	The dog kept scratching its ear.
31	quickly	Tegan can run quickly.
32	watch	Liam got a watch for his birthday.
33	sorry	Ted felt sorry for the lost dog.
34	learn	We have to learn our spelling for the test.
35	every	I eat vegetables every day.
36	through	Jason crawled through the tunnel.
37	possum	The possum had a baby.
38	goat	A baby goat is a kid.
39	goose	A baby goose is a gosling.
40	baking	Kim likes baking cakes.

Notes

Notes

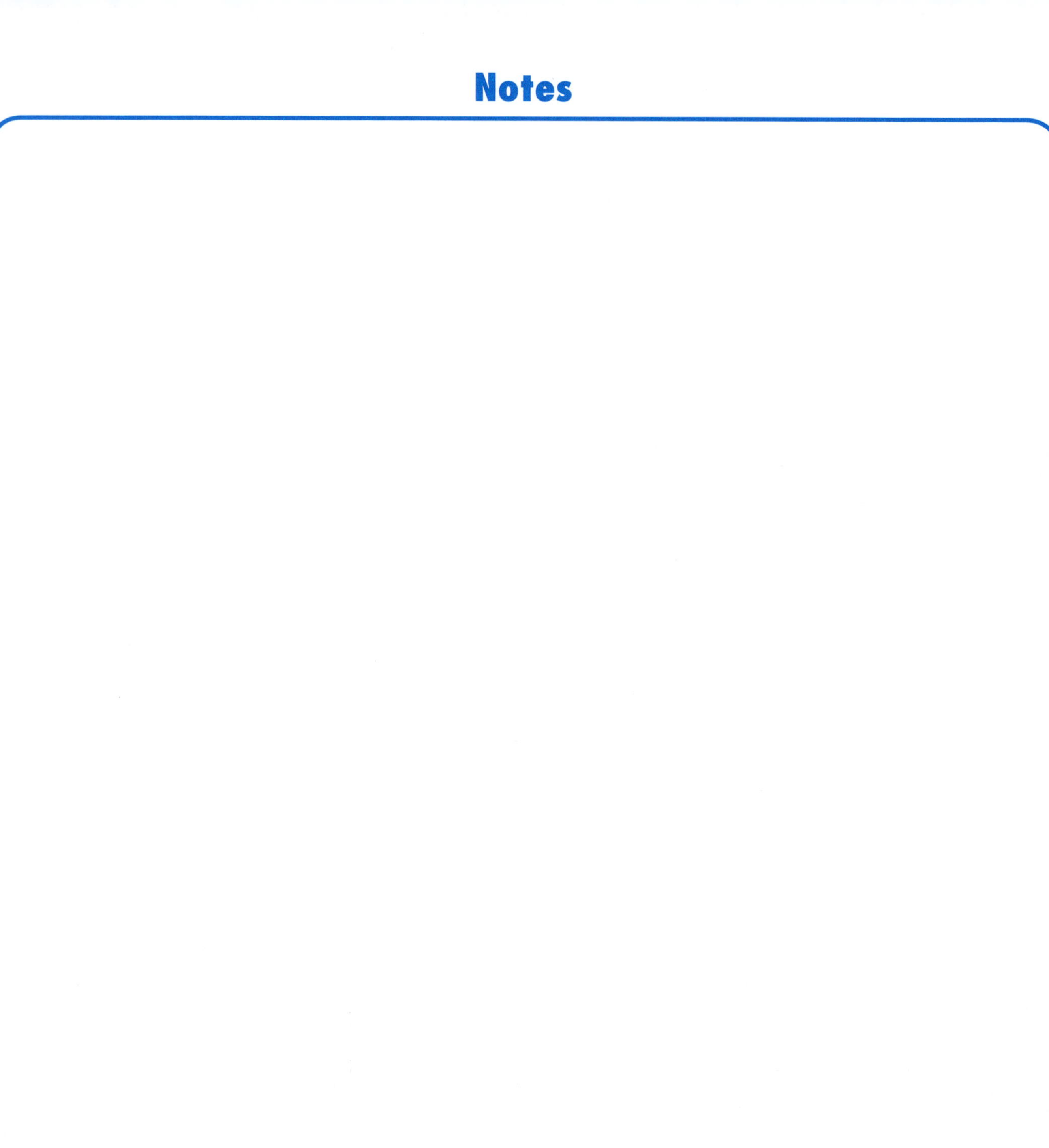